Urban and Regional Governance
in the Asia Pacific

Institute of Asian Research

THE UNIVERSITY OF BRITISH COLUMBIA
VANCOUVER, CANADA

Canadian Cataloguing in Publication Data

Main entry under title:

Urban and regional governance in the Asia Pacific

Includes papers from the conference, Urban Governance in Asia,
held in Taipei, March 10-14 1998.
Includes bibliographic references.
ISBN 0-88865-177-5

1. Local government--Pacific Area--Congresses. I. Friedmann,
John. II. University of British Columbia. Institute of Asian Research.
JS8450.U72 1999   320.8'09182'3   C99-910642-2

The Institute of Asian Research
The University of British Columbia
C.K. Choi Building, 1855 West Mall
Vancouver, British Columbia
Canada   V6T 1Z2

Table of Contents

Introduction

The selection of papers in this issue stems from a workshop on metropolitan governance in the Asia-Pacific region that was held in Taipei in April 1998. This was the second workshop involving a group of scholars from major cities of the region. With a common interest in urban policy, they call themselves the Intercity Network. The region itself, defined largely by trading patterns, extends from Japan and Korea down the coast of China to Southeast Asia, Australia, and North America. Overall, it presents what must surely be among the most challenging problems for urban policy in the world today. The region's cities are enormous in their scale and diversity. But the abstract vocabulary we commonly use to talk about them—sustainable growth, intercity competition, multicultural cities, metropolitan governance—lacks the conceptual precision and vividness with which to effectively communicate the awesome magnitude and specificity of the underlying realities.

The problematics confronting policy makers in the region's megacities are unprecedented. There are no relevant and robust theories to guide us into the future. Under these circumstances, urban policies must increasingly be thought of as so many explorations into *terrae icognitae*. We might think of them as unique experiments. The results of these policy experiments, regardless of how they may ultimately be judged, are not readily transferable, particularly from one country to others, and perhaps not even among cities within the same political-administrative space. But they are all we have to go on, and perhaps, if we look on them as "experiments," they might nudge us into a learning mode. We need carefully constructed maps of these explorations into an evolving urbanism, so that we can know where we have been, what we hoped to find, the paths by which we traveled, and the actual outcomes of our efforts. It is only by immersing ourselves into the specifics of these experiments, and in full awareness of their historical and cultural context, that we can use the recent past as a launching pad into an imagined future.

The essays that follow are about the governance of cities or, to be more precise, of large city-regions. Within the past few years, "governance" has become a fashionable tag, probably because of its emphasis, in a world of hyper-rapid change, on process. The dictionary tells us that governance refers to the "act, process or power of governing," and that it is also frequently used as a synonym for government. But its usage here, though pertinent to processes of governing, points *beyond* government to include all of the collective actors who might be brought into the system of managing a region. For any given city-region, actors may include the national state as well as provincial and local governments; international agencies such as the World Bank or the World Health Organization; multinational firms; and last but not least, organized civil society.[1] In very simplified form, we may think of governance processes as forming a triangle, involving state, capital, and civil society, the particular combination and the relative influence of each actor varying with political tradition and the purpose at hand. Thus, civil society plays a significant and growing role in the governance of cities in North America and Australia, but it is only just emerging in Asian societies (cf. for example, Brook and Frolic 1997). According to case studies reported by Chinese planners, for example, community participation in urban planning and decision-making is extremely limited. "In contrast to many rural Chinese communities where leaders are elected, leaders in urban areas are still appointed. Participation in urban governance in Chinese cities is largely passive: planners undertake opinion surveys, hold exhibitions during which citizens comment on plans and, in some cases, invite experts from different fields to interact with planners as projects near completion" (UNRISD 1998). What holds for China is valid, to a greater or lesser extent, for other countries in East and Southeast Asia as well. Even so, it will be useful to retain the image of a governance triangle, if only to be reminded of the potential presence of "civil associations, private sector organizations, community groups and social movements" in the process of urban management (McCarney, op. cit.).

The papers in this issue were written without a formal consensus on how to define governance. Some discussion of the concept took place during the workshop, but in writing their paper, each author proceeded to define just how they wanted to deal with their subject. What has emerged from this particular exploratory expedition is instructive, illustrating the great variety of tradition, procedure, and experience throughout our region.

John Friedmann leads off with a normative discussion of how one might assess urban governance in a perspective of civil society. Although not placed in a particular regional setting, the essay tacitly assumes a city, a

very large part of whose population does not share in the general pros-
perity. Contrary to "city benchmarking" which has lately become popular
as a way for cities to race each other in a competition for footlose global
capital, the essay asks searching questions about the performance of
cities: of political leadership and decision-making or governance proper,
of urban management in the implementation of policies, plans, and programs, and of outcomes. In this view, "governance," is to be evaluated on
three dimensions rather than for itself alone, with outcomes regarded as
important as the processes of reaching them.

The remaining studies all concern particular cities. The Murphy-Wu
paper on Sydney distinguishes managerial from entrepreneurial governance. Both are deeply influenced by Sydney's increasing insertion into
the global economy. Following a brief description of the Australian
federal system which lodges authority for urban decision-making with
the federal States while remaining financially dependent on the Commonwealth, the authors proceed to critically examine the two forms of
governance they have identified. On the managerial side, they look
specifically at the cost-recovery pricing of urban services and the privatization of urban development, including infrastructure. In the increasing
competition among Australian State capitals, Sydney being one of them,
the State government of New South Wales (which is the effective metropolitan planning agency for Sydney) has been forced into an aggressive
entrepreneurial role. Its capturing the Year 2000 Olympics is a case in
point. Entrepreneurialism has led the State into a close alliance with
business interests. The welfare effects of this response to inter-city
competition have not been all on the positive side, however, and
community resistance is growing.

Two papers on Korea follow. Won-Bae Kim focuses on conflicts in the
vast capital region of Seoul, while Dong-Ho Shin uses inter-
governmental (regional) conflicts centered on Pusan and Kyungnam province on the southeast coast. The two studies make an interesting pair,
revealing the enormous influence of the central government in local
governance. In Seoul, with its ten million people, current conflicts are
chiefly over land use controls which, the pro-business lobby argues, render
the region less competitive internationally. In Pusan, the "global" dimension of competition is swamped by conflict at both local and national
levels. Large Korean businesses are clearly vocal in both situations, while
civil society remainsfor the most part invisible, despite the stirrings of a
small environmental movement in Seoul.

Toshio Kamo reports on current debates on governance reforms in
Japan. His focus is on the Osaka-Kansai region, a powerful competitor to
Tokyo but lacking the latter's political clout. After working for decades

through a highly centralized system in which the national bureaucracy in Tokyo determined urban-regional policies and local governmental units were primarily there to ensure their correct implementation, the present financial-economic crisis is leading to a major rethinking of state-local relations. But the policies being proposed are contradictory. On the one hand, there is increasing recognition that effective power to make decisions should be decentralized. On the other, there is a belief that economies of scale can be achieved by consolidating both municipalities and prefectures (similar to American counties) and devolving powers to a small number of strong regional and perhaps enlarged metropolitan governments. Professor Kamo argues for a "post-Fordist" approach of flexibility, networking, and collaboration among existing local governments, the business community, and a nascent civil society as distinct from a formal restructuring of territorial powers.

An interesting and very different story is told by K.C. Ho who addresses the question of transborder governance in Southeast Asia. The city-state of Singapore, constrained by its territorial size, is organizing and investing in its hinterland in both Malaysia and Indonesia. Both of its neighboring countries are federations, but their central governments clearly dominate regional affairs, particularly when these involve international relations. At Singapore's instigation, a cooperative triangular arrangement was formed, officialized in 1994, that would facilitate the expansion of the Singaporean economy into the immediately adjacent areas of Johor State to the north and the Riau islands (which are part of Riau Province, the larger part of which is in Sumatra) to the south. The resulting economic region, dominated by Singaporean capital, is known by its acronym of SIJORI. Ho contrasts the peculiar form of governance that is emerging in this region with European and North American instances of transborder regional developments, and argues the case for a development authority to replace present bilateral arrangements.

A paper on Taiwan's fledgling civil society pertinent to the question of city-regional governance follows. In an imaginative piece, Lucie Cheng and Chu-joe Hsia contribute to the current political debates in Taiwan on constitutional reform, with a view to restructuring the forms of local governance on the island. The authors refer to their paper as a "strategy of writing rather than a prescriptive cure," and explicitly adopt a Daoist position as opposed to the Confucianism that informs mainstream thinking. "Putting it simply," they write, "the latter relies on the benevolence of the ruler, the former asks only to leave the people to govern themselves." This debate reminds one of the contrasting Jeffersonian and Hamiltonian views on governance in the writings surrounding the American Constitution.

The second half of their paper explores the transnational/transterritorial character of Taiwan's small but dynamic civil society. "What is new," they assert, "is the intense interconnectedness of individuals' lives across territories claimed by different states and other levels of government." Examples of transterritorial civil society in Taiwan include environmental, women's, and labor organizations. The authors conclude on a note of hope: "A transnationalized civil society, no longer containable within a territorial state, can strengthen the role of the civil society vis-à-vis its state in any particular country, Taiwan included."

Concluding this theme issue is Terry McGee's argument for a regional scale of governance, taking the Greater Vancouver Regional District as his example. Cities are embedded in larger functional regions, and criteria of good governance need to be applied at all scales, from the smallest local unit to more encompassing regional entities, allowing for the articulation of commonalities and differences. This is particularly important for the collectively consumed services such as transportation systems, water delivery and disposal, leisure areas and aspects of the environment such as air, etc. McGee argues that strategic planning for liveable urban regions will contribute to their attractiveness and make them more competitive as they engage in global competition to attract immigrants, tourists, capital and investment. Regional planning is one way of holding conflicts within manageable bounds and ensuring sustainable futures.

John Friedmann

Notes

[1]   McCarney specifically identifies "civic associations, private sector organizations, community groups and social movements, all of which in fact exert an indelible impact on the morphology and development of urban centres" (McCarney 1996, 5). She defines governance *exclusively* as the relationship between civil society and the state. The proposal here is to broaden the scope of governance to include all potential collective actors.

References

Brook, T. and B.M. Frolic, eds. 1997. *Civil Society in China*. Armonk, N.Y. and London: M.E. Sharpe.

McCarney, P.L., ed. 1996. *Cities and Governance: New Directions in Latin America, Asia, and Africa*. Toronto: University of Toronto, Centre for Urban and Community Studies.

UNRISD (United Nations Research Institute for Social Development). 1998. *UNRISD News*. 18 (Spring/Summer):16.

Preface

The Institute of Asian Research (IAR) at the University of British Columbia focuses on research and other activities under the Public Policy Program on contemporary, economic, political, social and technological change in Asia. One major policy issue is concerned by the management problems posed by the growth of mega-urban regions in Asia. Earlier research resulted in the publication of *The Mega-Urban Regions of Southeast Asia* (T.G. McGee and I. Robinson, eds., 1995).

The contents of this present book grew out of a workshop of an informal group of urban scholars from the some of the major cities in the Asia Pacific region known as the Intercity Network. The first workshop of this network was held at the Royal Melbourne Institute of Technology on 1-4 April 1997. The contents of the present volume grew out of the second meeting of the Intercity Network which took place at Taipei's Shih Hsin University from the 10-14 March 1998 with the financial assistance of the Taipei Municipal Government. Their support is gratefully acknowledged. This book was published with the financial support of the Ford Foundation.

The book cover was designed by Lisa Kwan who also proofread and designed the book. The editing production was carried out by Eleaanor Laquian. The assistance of Marietta Lau and Karen Jew in preparing manuscripts is also acknowledged. My thanks to them all for their highly professional work.

Terry McGee
Institute of Asian Research

JOHN FRIEDMANN

The Common Good:
Assessing the Performance of Cities*

T he question of the state has recently reappeared on the development agenda. After nearly three decades of neo-liberal rhetoric, in
which the state figured as Enemy No. 1, even the World Bank has
come around to acknowledge that, without a strong and active national
state, sustainable development is impossible. "An effective state," thus
the World Bank in its updated collective wisdom, "is vital for the provision of the goods and services—and the rules and institutions—that
allow markets to flourish and people to lead healthy and happier lives"
(World Bank 1997, 1).

Its *World Development Report* for 1997 is unquestionably a *tour-de-force*,
giving a detailed treatment of the state and its multiple failings in all the
major world regions. Not surprisingly, its focus is on the national state
(the number of United Nations member states stands currently at 185). I
say "not surprisingly" because the Bank, along with all other United Nations agencies, continues to believe in the mantra that economic development is best revealed in national statistics; it is the national state that
is invariably taken as the "natural" unit for analysis.

This picture is rapidly becoming obsolete, however. The actual
geography of the world economy is coming to resemble more and more
the geography of the United States, where it makes little sense to speak
of, say, the economy of a Rhode Island, North Dakota, or even California.
The states of the Union are so tightly interlinked that their economic
performance cannot be properly assessed *except as a function of these linkages*.

* *This paper was originally printed in a slightly different form in* Hemalata C. Dandekar
(*ed.*) (1998) City, Space & Globalization: An International Perspective. *Proceedings of an International Symposium, College of Architecture and Urban Planning,
University of Michigan, Ann Arbor. Grateful acknolwedgment is made to Hemalata
Dandekar for permission to print it here.*

This is not to argue that sub-national policy measures are unimportant, especially when they are focused on those metropolitan regions—a Boston, Miami, Chicago, Los Angeles, or Seattle—that serve as vital command centres, switching points, and global investment hubs through which the nation's economy is articulated into the global *space of flows* (Castells 1989, 1996). Quite to the contrary. What the World Bank has not yet dared to say is that the global space of flows is more accurately modeled by articulating it through a network of city-regions that function as the new core areas of the world economy (Sassen 1994; Knox and Taylor 1995; Friedmann 1996).

It follows that, important as is the role of national states in setting the institutional and policy parameters of all their developments, it is the governance of their major city-centred regions that will be decisive in how well they perform, not only in the global economy geared to capital accumulation but also in providing for the life and livelihood of their inhabitants. Perhaps the best way to understand the functioning of the actually existing world economy is not as an ensemble of 185 national states but as an archipelago of some 30 or 40 quasi-city-states that are linked to each other in a global system of economic, social, and political relations.

The question of good city governance is thus a direct counterpart of the question of governance posed by the World Bank at the level of the national state. While good governance nationally will undoubtedly benefit domestic city-regions, the performance of cities is not merely a reflection of structure and processes at the national level. We will have to look at the city-regional level on its own terms. And that is the premise with which I shall begin this paper.

Posing the Question

When shall we say that a city is well governed? Having posed this question leads me to ask two more. If governance concerns political process, what of a city's management—its ability to translate plans into action—and beyond that, what about the desired outcomes of good governance and good management? What should be the characteristics of a good city, which is our ultimate destination?

As Roger Keil has pointed out to me, this tripartite division is problematical because, so he argued, governance and management are intersecting, overlapping categories. Many government agencies wield more power than the city's executive authority or deliberative assembly; national ministries wield power over and may even preempt local decisions; and privatization has removed many traditional urban services from direct public scrutiny. The political moment and the bureaucratic moment, therefore, should not be separated.

This is no doubt a valid way of looking at the problem of "performance." I have nevertheless decided to retain the distinction. Although the concept of governance is inclusive of both corporate sector and organized civil society, it is the state that is ultimately responsible for political decisions and their outcomes. And it is the state's bureaucracy— its management arm—that is supposed to transpose political decisions into facts on the ground.

Taken together, my three questions pose the even broader issue of urban performativity. How well would any actually existing city or city-region stack up against criteria of good governance, good management, and good outcomes?

My questions raise major issues in political philosophy, but my deeper interests are practical. Given that our cities, especially our large cities in both the East and West, are in a sorry state—I do not wish to rehearse the litany of urban problems yet again—what shall we hold out as a vision, so that political practice (and planning) do not merely chase after problems, making small improvements here and there as opportunities arise, but move coherently toward an agenda of a truly human development? (For the current state of our cities, see United Nations Centre for Human Settlement 1996).

I am fully aware of the utopian character of any project that seeks a broad consensus around a vision of "the good city." Self-styled realists will argue that all we can ever hope to accomplish is to solve problems pragmatically with whatever resources are at hand. May they continue to do what they are doing. I will pitch my remarks to those who crave a different approach, who are not afraid to look beyond the visible horizon as a source of inspiration. We, too, want to be problem-solvers. The question is, how shall we define the problem so that, when we move toward ostensible solutions, we can be reasonably confident that, step-by-step, we are getting out of the woods rather than become more deeply entangled in the wilderness?

Economic Space, Life Space, Political Space

Up to now, I have used the term city in a very loose, general sense. On one hand, "city" can refer to a municipality. This is the simplest case. In other contexts, it can mean the densely built-up urban area, regardless of politico-administrative boundaries. But given the character of actual urbanization processes world-wide, I would like "city" to stand, at least at least for purposes of this essay, for the more encompassing concept of "city-region" that consists of a core city and its surrounding *urban field* which together constitute an *integrated functional/economic space* (Friedmann and Miller 1965; McGee 1995). Urban fields typically extend outward from the core to a distance of more than 100 km; they are the spaces into which the core city expands. They include the city's airports, new industrial estates, watersheds, recreation areas, water and sewage treatment facilities, intensive vegetable farms, outlying new urban districts, already existing smaller cities, power plants, petroleum refineries, and so forth, all of which are essential to the city's good functioning. City-regions on this scale can now have many millions of inhabitants, some of them rivalling medium-sized countries. This space of functional/economic relations may fall entirely within a single *political/administrative space* as is the case of the Hong Kong SAR and Toronto. More likely, however, it will cut across and overlap with a number—in some cases a very large number—of political-administrative spaces of cities, counties, districts, towns, provinces, etc. *Political/administrative space is the primary space of governance.*

Both spaces, functional/economic and political/administrative, overlie a set of smaller, loosely bounded, more intimately constructed spaces of social relation which I call *life space*. Life space is the space of everyday domesticity, of residentiary households in their social relations with neighbors, friends, family, and basic service providers. Often, it is centred on religious institutions and will typically include convenience stores, sport fields, pubs, local cafes, playgrounds, and parks. It will also be served, well or badly (or sometimes even not at all), by public facilities such as transportation, health posts, police posts, and the like. *Life space is the primary space of social reproduction.*

Although all three of these spaces can in principle be mapped, precise boundaries are often arbitrary, frequently blurred, and because of the internal dynamics of the city, may require repeated revisions to reflect continuous changes "on the ground." Moreover, cities do not exist in isolation but are interconnected with both nearby and distant, non-contiguous city-regions. *Cities form parts of systems of cities.*

The City as a Political Community, or Why a City is not a Hotel

Cities are real physical spaces in which our lives as urbanites unfold. The question that I now wish to pose is this: How do we relate, first, to the urban habitat; second, to our fellow urbanites; and third, to those in authority who claim to govern us? These three questions ultimately boil down to this: what does it mean to be an urban citizen?

In medieval Europe, to be a burgher was to be a citizen of a fortified city. Burghers were the inhabitants of a self-governing, chartered city and, as such, entitled to privileges not granted to the more numerous peasantry that served their feudal overlords in the surrounding countryside (Martines 1979; Braudel 1992). As the familiar saying went, "*Stadtluft macht frei*"—city air makes free—and this tradition of the city as a self-governing commune survives to this day: witness the loose association of some 70 major cities in the European Union that calls itself *Eurocities* and is engaged in cooperative research, information exchange, and policy coordination (Eurocities 1996).

Much has changed, of course, since self-governing cities first emerged in the European heartland during the 12th and 13th centuries. With the rise of the national state following the Treaty of Westphalia in 1648, cities lost much of their autonomy. The democratic revolution that began in the latter part of the 18th century and is still ongoing, resurrected the idea of citizenship but lodged it squarely in the national state, imagined as a sovereign political community. This weakening of city autonomy entailed a sharp decline of interest in local governance. In the United States, for example, where local councils are elected, citizen participation in local elections involves typically less than a third of those eligible to vote. Most people are content to pay their taxes and live in the city as though it were a hotel.

Let me elaborate on this metaphor and try to show where, I believe, it goes wrong. Let's assume that the city would, indeed, be like a hotel. As a hotel, it would be managed as most of them are, primarily in the interest of its well-paying guests who influence management and occupy the top floors of the tower, especially its penthouse suites. (The cheaper rooms are always in the lower stories, with single cubicles set aside for the poor in crowded basements, whilst numbers of homeless people jostle in the alleys behind the kitchen, feeding off food scraps). The management reports annually to a distinguished Board of (mostly male) Directors and an anonymous body of shareholders, most of whom have given their proxy vote to the Board. At these meetings, everyone's attention is focused on a single question: is the hotel profitable; what is its share of the local market; how can operating costs be further reduced?

Contrary to its glossy brochure, Hotel Metropole—which is what I shall call this run-down city hotel—is not the five-star facility it imagines itself to be. Although its management has become deeply corrupted, the elevators still work in a fashion, the water— increasingly of a dubious color—still runs from the faucets, the garbage still gets collected from most of the floors, albeit on an irregular schedule, the hallways are uncomfortably drab, smelly, and noisy. Over time, the hotel is getting ever more crowded, and new structures are being added haphazardly here and there. Guests are continually switching rooms: those who can afford it move up to higher floors which are reputed to have better service, others respond to the advertisements of competing hotels in the chain, still others move to different rooms on the same floor: there are rumors that things may be a bit more tolerable further down on this or that corridor. Despite increasingly appalling conditions, the Board of Directors has decided to keep the hotel running. Profits from its operations are helping to finance new hotels elsewhere. Hotel Metropole has become a cash cow.

What, if anything, is wrong with this story? The overall picture is surely a familiar one, and yet...something is not quite right. There are, in fact, three fatal flaws. No one can be said to "own" the city in the sense that stockholders own a capitalist enterprise[1]; cities are not supposed to be "profitable"; and many of the city's inhabitants, especially among the older generation, harbor strong attachments to the small corner of the earth that they regard as their "life space": the city, or at least their urban neighborhood or borough, forms a facet of their collective identity. But if the city is not a capitalist enterprise, and there is no distinguished Board of Directors, then what is it? And to whom should the city's management team report? If the city is not out to make a profit, then what purpose does it serve? And if the city's inhabitants are not paying "guests," then what are they, and what are their rights and obligations?

I shall cut directly to the core of my argument. In my view, the city is not a "hotel," because it is, potentially at least, a *political community*, a collective entity whose management is ultimately accountable to its long-term residents, its "citizens." In the final analysis, it is citizens who constitute its putative "Board of Directors," with the implicit power to "hire and fire" the city's management. A well-run city makes possible and enhances collective life. It creates the conditions for the integration of economic activities within the functional space it controls, and it supports the cluster of life spaces within which civil society and individual human lives flourish. The city's management can open up new economic and cultural opportunities and mediate conflict within the city's political space. But it is its residents who make the city productive. They constitute the city as a polity.

Nevertheless, I am aware that many, perhaps even most of us, would prefer to inhabit the city as though it were, indeed, something like a hotel. It would certainly be a lot more convenient. We may be long-suffering "guests," but getting involved in the mire and muck of urban politics is not worth the trouble with so many more immediately pressing or amusing things to do. In the United States, as I already mentioned, voter turnout in local elections is typically very low. People may grumble and complain but, so long as minimal services are provided, at least to their own neighborhoods, they remain largely unconcerned with the city as a political community.

Here, I shall argue for a more politically engaged position. The concept of *local citizenship*—practiced in a small federated republic such as Switzerland to this day— is not yet in currency world-wide, partly because citizenship is still thought to be tied exclusively to the national state. But this tight identity relation, nation=citizen, is beginning to crumble: in a dynamic, global economy, with mobile capital *and* labor, changing technologies, and shifting markets, multiple citizenship with all of its attendant ambiguities is becoming more and more the rule. In Europe, citizens of the European Union elect the parliament sitting in Strasbourg but they elect members of their own national legislatures as well: in some sense, they are already citizens of both, the European Union and their respective national states. Why should they then not also assert their right to be *local* citizens of the city or town where they reside?[2] And are we not, all of us, at least informally, already global citizens, concerned with world poverty issues, peace-keeping missions, the adjudication of international conflicts, global warming accords, species survival? Granted that global, macro-regional, national, and local claims on individuals may be in conflict, and this presents a practical, that is a political problem. But, whatever the difficulties in the specific case, I believe that formal recognition of local citizenship is now merely a matter of time.[3]

Some Preconditions for a Political Community

The concept of a political community and its associated ideas of (local) citizenship derive from the liberal democratic traditions of western Europe and North America, whose intellectual roots can be traced to ancient Greece, the Roman Republic, European humanism, and the democratic revolutions in the late 18th century in the American colonies and France (Skinner 1978). Although there were long centuries, even millennia, when democratic thought and practice were at low ebb, philosophers of the Enlightenment such as Locke, Montesquieu, Rousseau, Madison, J.S. Mill and others still carry a vital, contemporary message.

It is not my intention here to argue that democratic ideals are universally desirable, or indeed that they have ever been fully realized. Moreover, these ideals vary substantially, from those of liberal democracy on the right (Berlin 1969) to those of radical (participatory) democracy on the left (Barber 1984). Some uphold individualist, others more collective conceptions of justice as the foundation of political order (Walzer 1983; Young

1990). There are also important feminist perspectives (e.g., Pateman 1989). Political traditions follow different trajectories, and political systems in the Middle East and China, for example, would probably not support all of the performance criteria for cities I will propose in this essay. It remains to be seen to what extent, for example, Islamic or Confucian political traditions will devise performance criteria based on different principles (see, for example, Hsiao 1979; Du and Song 1995). Nevertheless, it is clear that democratizing forces are presently at work in many parts of the world outside the European heartland. The globalization of capital is partly responsible for this insofar as it is justified by an ideology of possessive individualism (MacPherson 1962) and requires the free circulation of information for its own long-term survival. Global media and the Internet are also contributing to this diffusion of political ideas. I shall therefore persist with my argument, leaving it for future resolution whether broadly democratic or some other set of criteria should be universally adopted (Davis 1995).

A political community, then, has *institutional correlates* without which it ceases to be a meaningful concept. I shall merely list a few of the major ones, since a full discussion is, in the present context, impossible. They include: universal suffrage and free periodic elections; freedom of speech, assembly, and association; freedom from arbitrary arrest; public media independent of state control; and a non-partisan legal system. It is these and similar conditions that make possible the vibrant life of a political community and undergird the role of citizens in the governance of cities.

Human Flourishing as a Universal Human Right

Allow me now to return to my main topic. Criteria for assessing the performance of cities require a normative foundation without which any further discussion would become incoherent. These founding principles should be so clearly formulated that they can be communicated even to people who are not philosophically inclined but make their living as carpenters, domestic workers, or construction workers. As a norm, they must also be powerful and persuasive enough to serve as a beacon for governance and public policy. Here is how I would formulate this foundational value:

> Every human being has the right, by nature, to the full development of their innate intellectual, physical, and spiritual potentialities in the context of wider communities.

I call this the *right to human flourishing*. It has never been universally acknowledged as an inherent right of being human. Slave societies knew nothing of it; nor did caste societies, tribal societies, corporate village societies, or totalitarian states. And in no society have women ever enjoyed the same right to human flourishing as men. But as the fundamental right of every person, human flourishing is implicit in the democratic ethos.

Human flourishing underlies the strongly held belief in contemporary western societies that privilege should be earned rather than I inherited. Human beings should accordingly have an equal start in life. Over a life time, individual and group outcomes will, of course, vary because of differences in innate abilities, family upbringing, entrenched privilege, class formation, social oppression, and other reasons. Still, the idea of a basic equality among all of their citizens underlies the mild socialism of western countries with their systems of public education, public health, the graduated income tax, anti-discriminatory legislation, etc., all of which seek some sort of leveling of life chances among individuals and groups.

The Common Good

It would be foolish, however, to insist, as Margaret Thatcher did when she reportedly dismissed the notion of "society" as a fiction, that human flourishing is largely or even primarily an individual achievement, independent of any social context. Flourishing does not depend on us alone as individuals—it is not only a matter of individual achievement— for the simple reason that we are all profoundly social beings as well. As individuals ultimately responsible for our actions, we are constrained in what we do by (1) our social relations with family, friends, work mates, and neighbors, in short, by an ethics of mutual obligation within civil society and (2) the social settings of our lives, by which I mean the set of socially produced *conditions* that may and often do inhibit human flourishing. Although the first set of constraints can be very powerful indeed, I will not further address it here because, for the most part, it lies outside the public sphere. Rather, I will turn to the second set which is the primary focus of this essay.

Briefly, my argument is that local citizens do not merely *use* the city to advance their personal interests—some will do so more successfully than others—but also contribute, as members of their political community, which is the city in its political aspect, to establish and maintain *the basic conditions—political, economic, social, and physical—for the human flourishing of all citizens of the community*. I refer to these basic conditions as the *common good* of the polity, or the *good city*, because without them, human flourishing would be impossible. The "common good" therefore implies something akin to *citizen rights*, that is, to the rightful claims that any local citizen can make on her or his political community based on the inalienable right to human flourishing.

The "common good" may sound like a concept coming from an earlier, more benign era. In a neo-liberal age and a globalizing economy, where the untrammeled pursuit of self-interest has been raised to the level of an unassailable virtue, it has a distinctly old-fashioned ring. While neo-conservatives in the West raise the banner of individualism unconstrained by social obligations, progressives decry the "common good" as a rhetorical trick of the hegemonic class that merely serves to hide their own class interest. Post-modern critics, for their part, argue that ours is an era of social fragmentation, and that meta-narratives proposing to offer a basis for social coherence are simply no longer possible (Tagg 1996). Their refuge is a regressive aestheticism. Against neo-liberals, political progressives, and post-modernists, I would argue that a political community has no purchase except as it invokes a conception of the "common good." Unless we can agree that a common good can be defined, at least in principle and for a given social formation, we would have to be content with our fable of the Hotel Metropole. We would have to be satisfied to live as "guests" in a city on which we have no special claims.

Toward Criteria for Assessing the Performance of Cities

Let me review the logic of my argument so far. I have posited human flourishing as a universal human right. To make this right operational, certain conditions of a political, economic, social, physical, and environmental character must exist. Although these conditions are, in principle, enabling, they also impose social constraints on the individual. The primary site for establishing/creating these conditions is the city, constituted as a political community. In this context, the right to human flourishing appears as a right that can be claimed by local citizens. Becoming a member of a political community, and thus an active local citizen, should be facilitated for newcomers to the city.

Continuing this line of argument, the facilitating conditions for human flourishing must be available on an equal basis to all citizens who, in turn, assume a civic obligation to help bring about and sustain these conditions. Although this equality principle is unassailable as such, the unequal treatment of women, ethnic and religious groups, lower castes, the invisible underclass, and groups marked by certain phenotypical characteristics is a fact in virtually every major city of the

world. As a principle in the political order, however, egalitarianism cannot by itself dissolve the remaining, stubborn inequalities in the civil
order. In addition to the formal declaration of rights in the political order,
therefore, a concurrent struggle must take place to secure an equality of
rights in the civil order as well.

An unresolved question concerns the correct balance between
individual, self-interested striving and one's obligations toward groups
and collectivities, including one's political community. The Anglo-Saxon
variety of capitalism has always leaned far to the side of individualism,
leaving little more than a yearning for community among many people.
Socially, it has been a disaster. Chinese communism of the Mao Ze Dong
variety leaned far in the other direction, where the demands of the
collectivity all but swallowed up individual striving. It, too, was a disaster.
The golden mean obviously lies in the difficult balance between the one
and the many. The problem is that whatever equilibrium between
self-advancement and social obligation may be momentarily attained, it
will never be a stable one. At present, there is considerable debate in the
United States about the importance of so-called family-values,
communitarianism, and relations within civil society based on trust,
face-to-face relations, and mutuality, often referred to as *social capital*
(Putnam 1993). However, mainstream America continues to be enthralled
by the promise of an unfettered individualism and fails to connect its
rampant and pervasive problems of social alienation to the absence of
precisely this lack of social engagement, this blind denial of the social
nature of human beings and the deeply felt human needs that spring
from that source.

Defining the Criteria

I now turn to the identification of the criteria for assessing the performance of cities. As I hinted at the start, criteria can be divided into three
groups: good governance, good management, and good outcomes. *Good
city governance* refers to the political processes of allocating resources and
"steering" the collective life of the political community. It involves the
triad of state, corporate sector, and civil society joined in various forms
of collaborative local action.[4] *Good city management* concerns the administration and use of common resources in bringing about those minimal
conditions of urban life that make possible individual human flourishing. Finally, *good city outcomes* concern those which further the common
good of the city, including the strengthening of good governance, thereby
completing the circle.

The specific criteria I would propose follow below.

I. Criteria of Good City Governance

- *inspired political leadership*: leaders capable of articulating a common vision for the polity, building a strong consensus around this vision, and mobilizing resources toward its realization.
- *public accountability*:
  (1) the uncoerced, periodic election of political representatives and
  (2) the right of local citizens to be adequately informed about those who stand for elections, the government's performance record, and the overall outcomes for the city (see III below).
- *inclusiveness*: the right of all citizens to be directly involved in the formulation of policies and programs whenever consequences are expected significantly to affect their life and livelihood.
- *responsiveness*: the fundamental right of citizens to claim rights and express grievances; to appropriate channels for this purpose; to a government that is accessible to people in their neighborhoods and districts; and to an acknowledgment by government that citizens' claims and grievances require an attentive, appropriate response.
- *non-violent conflict management*: refers to institutionalized methods of resolving conflicts between the state and its citizens without resorting to physical violence.

II. Criteria of Good City Management

- *accessibility, transparency, responsiveness*: the city bureaucracy should be equally accessible to citizens from all walks of life, transparent in its manner of operation, and responsive to citizen complaints and initatives.
- *effectiveness*: programs launched to attain specific, politically-sanctioned results should also come close to achieving them. Privatized urban services should be carefully monitored for their compliance with performance standards.
- *efficiency*: in striving for maximum effectiveness, government-sponsored programs should use resources as efficiently as possible.
- *honesty*: in carrying out public programs, all concerned parties should be treated fairly, without favoritism. Basically, this criterion speaks to the honesty and incorruptibility of public officials.

III. Criteria of Good City Outcomes

- a *productive* city: provides the right to adequately remunerated work for those who seek it.

- a *sustainable* city: ensures the right to a life-sustaining and life-enhancing natural environment for every citizen, now and in the future.
- a *liveable* city: guarantees all citizens their right to decent housing and associated public services, including health and personal safety, in the neighborhoods of their choice.
- a *safe* city: ensures each person's right to the physical integrity and security of their body.
- an *actively tolerant city*: protects and promotes citizen rights to group-specific differences in language, religion, national custom, sexual preference, and similar markers of collective identity, so long as these do not invade the rights of others and are consistent with more general human rights.
- a *caring* city: acknowledges the right of the weakest members of the polity to adequate social provision.

I call this listing of criteria a *minimum agenda* for the "good city."⁵ Although it does not place extraordinary demands on existing institutions, it does entail a vibrant civil society, an active praxis of democratic citizenship, and an independent press prepared to support responsible, investigative journalism. These are the preconditions before the "good city" can make an appearance. Once these preconditions are met, however, how should the criteria be used, and by whom, toward what end? First, I want to emphasize what I would consider to be an inappropriate use. The criteria of good city governance, management, and outcomes are not designed for a comparative analysis of city performance. To look for and construct quantitive indicators by which to measure and compare city performance would be a misguided effort, for two reasons. Even if it were possible to construct plausible indicators for each criterion, it would be impossible to combine them into an aggregate performance index for the simple reason that there will never be agreement on the relative weighting of the separate criteria. Secondly, quantitative indicators are normally read as standing for the whole which they are supposed to "indicate," but such a reading would be invalid in this case. A tolerant city cannot be adequately measured, say, by the number of violent acts committed against so-called minority groups. Whereas reducing violence against certain sectors of the population may become an immediate objective in one situation (though not necessarily in others), it cannot replace the continuing search for a more actively tolerant city everywhere, which will always have a more encompassing meaning than can possibly be captured by any single indicator or set of indicators. What is needed in place of performance indicators is *a critical, narrative account* of the way that the civil and political rights of different

socially and culturally specific groups are adequately protected and promoted in a given city.

No actually existing city would score high on all of the criteria I have
enumerated; no city is ever likely to be called a "good city." But every city
can try to better itself on some dimension of its performance. The criteria
are thus intended to be used by the citizens of each city—its organized
civil society—as a tool for mapping the existing states of affairs, and for
setting an agenda for civic struggle and action (Douglass and Friedmann
1998). For I believe that it is, in principle, possible to obtain substantial
agreement among the general population on criteria that propose to tell
us what we have the right to hope for in a "good city."

Acknowledgments

I wish to thank Roger Keil, Brian Howe, Rebecca Abers, and Leonie
Sandercock for their thoughtful reading of earlier drafts of this paper and
for their many useful suggestions for its improvement. Responsibility for
the present text remains, of course, entirely mine.

Notes

[1] But see Isin (1992) for the contrary review that modern cities in Europe
and North America are best understood as corporations.

[2] Denmark is one European country where even non-Danish nationals
obtain the right to vote in local elections after a residency of three
years (Garcia 1996).

[3] See Held (1995) for a similar argument.

[4] There are numerous attempts to define "governance." But a core
meaning to all is the conjoining of state and civil society in the process
of making decisions in the public domain (McCarney 1996). To this
dyadic formulation, I have added as equally indispensible the corporate
sector, thus forming a triad. See Berg (1993).

[5] In the April 1998 Asia-Pacific Intercity Network workshop on urban-
regional governance held in Taipei, where I presented this paper,

Professor Won-Bae Kim pointed out that my "good city" criteria concerned citizens rights to the exclusion of obligations. I concur with this observation. On reflection, however, I would venture the following generalization. Whereas western political theory is, indeed, primarily a theory of individual rights, east Asian philosophy has elaborated a complex theory of obligations. First articulated in the *Analects* of Confucius, the latter is based on a "bottom-up" system of reciprocal obligations (i.e., beginning with familial relations) that extend, step by step, all the way to the King or Emperor (the state). A correlative theory of rights is foreign to this conception, just as rights theory (as formulated, for example, in the U.S. Bill of Rights) has little to offer on the question of citizen responsibilities. The Bill of Rights is essentially the individual citizen's principled line of defense against the encroachments of the state. Such a conception is difficult to graft onto Chinese political theory.

References

Barber, B.R. 1984. *Strong Democracy: Participatory Politics for a New Age*. Berkeley: University of California Press.

Berg, L. van den, H.A. van Klink and J. van der Meer 1993. *Governing Metropolitan Regions*. Aldershot, U.K.: Ashgate.

Berlin, I. 1969. *Four Essays on Liberty*. New York: Oxford University Press.

Braudel, F. 1992. *The Perspective of the World*. Vol. III of Civilization and Capitalism, 15th-18th Century. Berkeley: University of California Press.

Castells, M. 1996. *The Rise of the Network Society*. Oxford: Blackwell.

Castells, M. 1989. *The Informational City: Information Technology, Economic Restructuring, and the Urban-Regional Process*. Oxford: Blackwell.

Davis, M.C., ed. 1995. *Human Rights and Chinese Values: Legal, Philosophical, and Political Perspectives*. Hong Kong: Oxford University Press.

Douglass, M. and J. Friedmann, eds. 1998. *Cities for Citizens: Planning and the Rise of Civil Society in a Global Age*. Chichester: John Wiley and Sons.

Du, G. and G. Song. 1995. Relating Human Rights to Chinese Culture: the Four Paths of the Confucian Analects and the Four Principles of a New Theory of Benevolence. *Human Rights and Chinese Values*. Edited by M. Davis. Hong Kong: Oxford University Press.

Eurocities. 1996. A *Charter of the European Cities: Towards a Revision of the Treaty on European Union*. Brussels.

Friedmann, J. 1996. *World City Futures: The Role of Urban and Regional Policies in the Asia-Pacific Region*. Occasional Paper 56. Hong Kong: Hong Kong Institute of Asia-Pacific Studies, The Chinese University of Hong Kong.

Friedmann, J. and J. Miller. 1965. The Urban Field. *Journal of the American Institute of Planners*. November: 312-319.

Garcia, S. 1996. Cities and Citizenship. *International Journal of Urban and Regional Research*. 20, 1 (March): 7-21.

Held, D. 1995. *Democracy and the Global Order: From the Modern State to Metropolitan Governance*. Cambridge: Polity Press.

Hsiao, K.-C. 1979 (1954). A *History of Chinese Political Thought*. Vol. 1: *From the Beginnings to the Sixth Century*. Princeton: Princeton University Press.

Isin, E.F., 1992. *Cities without Citizens: The Modernity of the City as a Corporation*. Montreal, New York: Black Rose Books.

Knox, P.L. and P.J. Taylor, eds. 1995. *World Cities in a World System*. Cambridge University Press.

McCarney, P.L. 1996. *Cities and Governance: New Directions in Latin America, Asia and Africa*. Toronto: Centre for Urban and Community Studies, University of Toronto.

McGee, T.G. 1995. Retrofitting the Emerging Mega-Urban Regions of ASEAN: An Overview. *The Mega-Urban Regions of Southeast Asia*. Edited by T.G. McGee and I.M. Robinson. Vancouver: University of British Columbia Press.

MacPherson, C.B. 1962. *The Political Theory of Possessive Individualism. Hobbes to Locke*. Oxford University Press.

Martines, L. 1979. *Power and Imagination: City-States in Renaissance Italy*. New York: Alfred A. Knopf.

Pateman, C. 1989. *The Disorder of Women: Democracy, Feminism and Political Theory*. Stanford: Stanford University Press.

Putnam, R.D. 1993. *Making Democracy Work: Civic Traditions in Modern Italy*. Princeton: Princeton University Press.

Sassen, S. 1994. *Cities in a World Economy*. Thousand Oaks, London, New Delhi: Pine Forge Press.

Skinner, Q. 1978. *The Foundations of Mosdern Political Thought*. 2 vols. Cambridge: Cambridge University Press.

Tagg, J. 1996. The City Which Is Not One. *Re-presenting the City: Ethnicity, Capital and Culture in the 21st-Century Metropolis*. Edited by A.D. King. New York: New York University Press.

United Nations Centre for Human Settlements (Habitat). 1996. *An Urbanizing World: Global Report on Human Settlements*. Oxford University Press.

Walzer, M. 1983. *Spheres of Justice*. New York: Basic Books.

World Bank. 1997. *The State in a Changing World: World Development Report 1997*. Oxford University Press.

Young, I. 1990. *Justice and the Politics of Difference*. Princeton: Princeton University Press.

PETER A. MURPHY AND CHUNG-TONG WU

Governing Global Sydney: From Managerialism to Entrepreneurialism

In common with cities world wide, metropolitan Sydney has become intricately enmeshed in the processes of globalization over the past quarter-century. As an outcome, the management of growth and change in the city has become more challenging and increasingly co-opted to economic development. This paper demonstrates how Sydney's governance has been influenced by its incorporation into the global economy. First, key substantive aspects of the metropolitan region, especially the legal and financial frameworks that underpin its governance, are outlined. Second, contemporary trends and outcomes in Sydney's governance, and their connections with economic globalization, are explored. Third, welfare implications of globally driven shifts in governance are considered. Whilst the paper is not explicitly concerned with how the impacts of globalization have been modulated by local circumstance a number of examples are implicit in the text. Figure 1 summarizes the argument and may be read both as an introduction and as a conclusion to the paper.

Three key notions—*city planning, urban governance* and *globalization*—are used in the paper. In the interests of brevity it is assumed that readers of this journal will be familiar with the concepts of globalization. Regarding *governance*, a first point to note is that it is not simply the provenance of elected governments but rather the outcome of influences from business and civil society (essentially NGOs) acting upon elected governments. The presumption is that such influences are increasing in scale and complexity. Studies of urban governance have been revitalized in recent years due in large measure to changes wrought by the growth of the new entrepreneurialism. At the more pragmatic and empirical end of the spectrum of new urban political theory, much attention has been paid to "growth coalitions" (e.g. Newman and Thornley 1997; Harding 1994). These consist of loose or informal partnerships of a multiplicity of interest groups which function together in order to make and carry out "governing"

Figure 1: Reduction of Government Financial Capacity, Mangerial and Entrepreneurial Governance

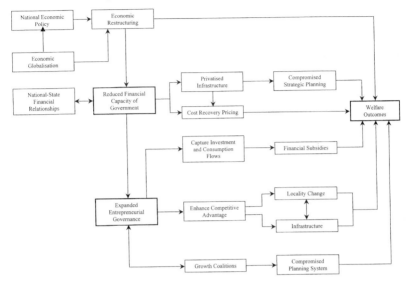

decisions. "Members" of such coalitions typically include: property interests; rentiers; utility groups; universities; business groups; trade unions; and media.

At a deeper level, "regulationist" forms of social analysis have attempted to incorporate "the urban" into new models of regulation of the process of capitalist accumulation. In particular, "regime theory has been regarded as an appropriate means of interpreting the changing complexion of urban politics. [It posits that] the ability of city governments to shape urban futures and development needs to be understood in terms of the social production of governance" (Hall and Hubbard 1996, 155). From this perspective, it is not so much a matter of who governs officially but who has the capacity to act and why. Regime theory thus transcends simplistic views posited by elitist and pluralist theories of urban governance. In so doing it also de-constructs the notion that only electoral power creates leverage.

A key distinction in contemporary studies of urban governance is between *managerialism* and *entrepreneurialism*. Managerialism refers to the practices of "good housekeeping," that is regulation of land use, environmental management and infrastructure provision. Such practices may be regarded as the conventional tasks of urban governance. Entrepreneurialism refers to initiatives by the state to capture geographically mobile investment and consumption flows or to otherwise boost a

city's economy. Hall and Hubbard (1996, 154) note that "urban politicians and governors are increasingly arguing that cities can benefit not
only from "conventional" welfare measures or land-use planning but by
mobilizing local resources in the scramble for rewards in an increasingly
competitive free market." Moreover, these "new" modes of governance
are characterized by "the promotion of local economic development by
urban governments, typically in alliance with private capital" (p.154).

David Harvey (1989, 22-23) argued that governments can lure mobile
and flexible production, financial and consumption flows in three ways.
First they can use their capacity to produce goods and services for local
use or export. This may involve pressuring local labor forces to keep costs
down and eliminate disruptive industrial action. Governments can also
invest in infrastructure such as airports and telecommunications systems,
or they can offer direct state financial support for business in the form of
tax holidays, loan guarantees and the like. A second strategy is to make
cities better places to live and do business by building sophisticated
recreational complexes or by the propagation of good urban design in its
many forms. A third strategy is to attract "command and control functions" of transnational corporations and associated producer services
complexes and join the global city stage (cf. Sassen 1991).

Whilst political processes and the structure of government unquestionably frame and constantly interact with city planning systems, it is
nevertheless possible to separate out *planning* as a set of technical and
micro-political actions. In its modernist conception planning is a state
function focusing on regulating land use and activity location in the "public
interest." Planning is regarded as essentially technocratic but with
frequent and obvious political interventions. The post-modernist project
focuses on space in a looser, more holistic sense. In this paradigm
planning is regarded as essentially a process of empowerment (see, for
example, Sandercock 1998, for a compelling representation of this view
of planning). This conception has its roots in community planning rather
than town planning as the terms would be understood in Australia.

The Sydney Metropolitan Region

Sydney is the largest city in Australia and capital of the state of New
South Wales (NSW). Its population—approaching 4 million—represents
20 percent of the Australian total. The city houses 60 percent of the NSW
total population and thus dominates the state's economic and political
activities. Sydney is also Australia's most globalized city (Murphy and
Watson 1997; NSW Department of State and Regional Development 1997;
NSW Tourism Strategy 1997). It has much higher shares of regional head-

quarters (RHQs) of transnational corporations than its strongest Australian competitor city, Melbourne. It hosts headquarters and RHQs of three-quarters of international and domestic banks. It has Australia's largest stock exchange and the only futures exchange in Australia. Currently, of the top 500 corporations in Australian and New Zealand, 228 are headquartered in Sydney and 127 in Melbourne (NSW Department of State and Regional Development 1997). Sydney also captures twice as many international tourist nights as Melbourne. High levels of immigration are also indicators of globalization and Sydney has gained a disproportionate share of immigrants in recent years, especially from Asian sources (see Table 1).

Sydney's competitive advantage over other Australian cities derives from its being the hub of international traffic into and out of Australia, its environmental amenity (climate, harbor, beaches, topography) and its multicultural population. It now gains cumulative advantage from having captured disproportionate shares of growth generating investment and consumption flows over the past quarter of a century. Compared with competitor cities in east and southeast Asia, Sydney's competitive advantage derives from environmental amenity, cheap professional labor and low rents for housing and commercial floor space.

Australian cities differ in important respects from those in other parts of the advanced capitalist world, especially North America. A key contrast is the tendency toward lower incomes in outer city areas of high population growth, combined with low numbers of jobs per capita in those same regions (Australian Bureau of Statistics 1998). This combination of circumstances produces long average journeys to work, disproportionately by private automobile, for many outer city residents (NSW Government 1991). A major factor behind high levels of air pollution, this spatial

Table 1: Capital City Shares of Growth in Australian Population and Overseas-born Persons, 1971 to 1991

City	Share of Population Growth (%)	Share of Growth in Overseas-Born (%)
Sydney	14.4	30.1
Melbourne	11.7	17.2
Perth	10.5	13.6
Brisbane	3.6	5.6
Adelaide	4.2	2.6

Source: Australian Bureau of Stastics, Population and Housing Censuses

configuration is also implicated in disproportionately high levels of un-employment that characterize large parts of the Australian outer city (Australian Bureau of Statistics 1998; Vipond 1985).

Air and water pollution are more significant problems in Sydney than in other Australian capital cities (Commonwealth State of the Environment Report 1996). This is substantially a by-product of Sydney's pre-eminence as Australia's largest city, since with production and consumption patterns constant, as they more or less are across Australia, pollution is ultimately a matter of numbers. Local circumstances add significantly to the problem because Sydney is sited in a topographic basin, with high land to south, west and north; the Tasman Sea forms an eastern boundary. Ventilation by prevailing winds is accordingly weak. Water pollution results from sewage and storm water disposal through ocean outfalls to the east and to the Hawkesbury-Nepean River to the west. Since most of Sydney's population growth is in the catchment of this river system water quality problems are acute (NSW Department of Urban Affairs and Planning 1997).

From its superior competitive status compared with other Australian cities, its population size, environmental and social characteristics it may be expected that in Sydney, managerial challenges will be most forcefully felt and entrepreneurial opportunities most bountiful. Because of the intrinsic similarities of the larger Australian cities Sydney serves, however, as an exemplar of contemporary managerial and entrepreneurial initiatives and structures of Australian urban governance.

Structure of Urban Government

1. *Powers and responsibilities of commonwealth, state and local government in relation to land use and activity location*
The commonwealth (Australian) government lacks constitutional authority to intervene directly in the governance of the cities. Indirectly it has the capacity to influence events through direct funding of programs administered by the states, by construction of commonwealth-owned infrastructure and through policies that impact on the cities as by-products. Commonwealth interest in urban affairs waxes and wanes. Politically conservative governments—such as the one in power at time of writing—are typically uninterested in urban affairs and are content to regard them as state responsibilities.

It is state governments that have the constitutional authority to regulate land use and activity location in the cities. In addition, although there has been a pronounced trend to corporatization and privatization (see below), urban infrastructure has traditionally been provided by state agencies. In New South Wales, the central planning agency is the Department of Urban Affairs and Planning (DUAP). Whilst it has statewide responsibilities, it is effectively the metropolitan planning agency for Sydney. In Australia, local government also has a regulatory and strategic planning role but is circumscribed by state legislation. The NSW Environmental Planning and Assessment Act (EPAA) delineates the powers of state and local government in relation to land use planning.

II. *Financial capacities of, and arrangements between, levels of government*

Australian state and local governments historically constructed and debt-financed urban infrastructure. For three reasons, however, their capacity to continue operating in this manner diminished over the past quarter century (Kirwan 1990). First, higher long-term interest rates resulted from the global explosion of demand for capital. Second, replacement and refurbishment needs, largely unplanned for, emerged since much urban infrastructure is old, such as water and sewerage mains, and inner city roads that were not at all designed to accommodate current volumes of traffic. Third, environmental degradation created demand for new forms of urban infrastructure. If degradation is to be arrested it requires—along with regulatory and pricing reform—investment in urban infrastructure such as sewage treatment works and public transport. In addition to these factors, in Australia, and to varying degrees in the rest of the western industrialized world, slowed rates of economic growth since the early 1970s have limited growth in per capita tax revenues and thus exacerbated difficulties faced by governments charged with infrastructure provision.

An important feature of the story of urban infrastructure provision in Australia (and elsewhere) is that governments historically financed it only partly from charges levied on users. Resource costs of provision have thus been substantially met from general taxation revenue. The pressures just noted have led governments to privatize provision or to charge prices that bear a closer relationship to costs of construction and maintenance. An aspect of this relates to "externalities" (social costs), such as air and water pollution, which evidence under-priced environmental resources.

A key issue in the Australian context concerns financial relationships between federal, state and local governments. Urban public infrastructure is overwhelmingly constructed, maintained and financed by state and local governments with varying levels of direct cost recovery from users. "In 1991, the States were responsible for 62 per cent of national capital spending on infrastructure [urban and otherwise], compared to the Commonwealth with 24 per cent of spending responsibilities and Local Government with 14 per cent" (Commonwealth Industry

Commission 1993, 12). A feature of the perennial bargaining that goes on between state and commonwealth governments turns on the fact that the commonwealth operates programs—such as immigration—that impact on the cities. There is thus continuing debate as to whether the commonwealth redistributes sufficient taxation revenue to cover costs accrued by the "lower" levels of government.

The commonwealth government—due to its monopoly over personal and company income taxes—raises more revenue than it requires for its own operations. State governments, in contrast, raise only around half of what they need from their own sources. Revenue is returned to the states in the forms of General Revenue and Specific Purpose Payments (Commonwealth Grants Commission 1995). One issue for the states is the total quantum of revenue that is provided; another is the method of distribution used by the commonwealth. The total quantum returned to the states has been dropping in real terms as the commonwealth government has sought to balance its own books.

In 1994-95, A$17.7 billion worth of General Revenue Grants were returned to the states. The funds are distributed so as to enable an equal quality of services to be provided by the states, irrespective of their own financial capacity and the scale of task involved (Commonwealth Grants Commission 1993). This is the so-called principle of "fiscal equalization" that accounts for wide disparities in per capita grants from the commonwealth to the states (see Table 2).

In the current period of fiscal constraint in Australia, the politics of state-federal financial relations mean that states are especially pressured to use whatever arguments are at hand to lever more money from the

Table 2: Financial Assistance Grants from Commonwealth to States, A$ per capita, 1989-90 and 1991-92

State	1989-90	1991-92
New South Wales	628	611
Victoria	619	601
Queensland	844	880
Western Australia	920	949
South Astralia	971	1020
Tasmania	1101	1196
Northern Territory	4134	4492

Source: NSW Budget paper No. 2 (1989 & 1991)

commonwealth. NSW and Victoria, in particular, note higher per capita payments to the less populous states and argue that, whilst these may have been justified in earlier decades, they are no longer reasonable.

Whilst modest in its responsibilities compared with state governments, local government in Australia does provide a wide range of urban infrastructure and services, including local roads and drainage systems, libraries, child care facilities and the like. Compared with other countries though, notably the USA, local government's role is residual and, as noted above, accounts for only 14 percent of national spending on infrastructure. The fact that urban infrastructure and public services are primarily supplied by the states is important. It means that the size of local tax bases is a much less important determinant of service availability and quality—and therefore peoples' welfare—than it is in some other parts of the world (Murphy and Watson 1994). The financial capacity of local government has nevertheless been limited for several years with rate (property tax) increases—the main source of revenue—being capped below inflation by fiat from state governments.

The commonwealth contributes directly to local government to varying degrees across states under the Commonwealth Local Government (Financial Assistance) Act 1995 and its predecessors. In 1995-96, A$1.16 billion was distributed under this arrangement although, proportional to national GDP, this amount has been declining since the early 1980s (NSW Local Government Grants Commission 1995). Funds are distributed through state governments to local government councils according to formulae devised by state Local Government Grants Commissions. Financial Assistance Grants as a proportion of local government revenue accordingly range from less than 3 percent to over 20 percent among, for example, Sydney councils. Differential needs and capacity to raise revenue from local property taxes account for the differences.

From Managerialism to Entrepreneurialism

Until the 1970s managerialist concerns were the focal point of Sydney's governance. These days, whilst such concerns are as important as always, entrepreneurialism has added to the complexity of managerial governance as well as being a pronounced feature of governance in its own right. This part of the paper first reviews the nature and implications of changes in managerialist governance that have: shifted infrastructure provision from the public to the private sector; maintained public provision but increasingly on a cost-recovery basis; and increased the exercise of state power over local government in relation to land-use regulation. The emergence of entrepreneurial governance is then examined.

Challenges to Managerial Governance

I. *Privatized provision of urban infrastructure*

As is the case internationally, Australian state and local governments are stepping away from supplying urban infrastructure and services, or else are instituting cost-recovery pricing arrangements (which, from a consumer's viewpoint, amounts to the same thing). These are direct outcomes of financial pressures imposed on governments by economic globalization. They are, however, politically fraught, since they imply higher prices to some consumers and because a significant proportion of the Australian electorate supports public ownership of key capital assets

Pertinent in the context of a paper dealing with urban governance is the potential for privatization to "corrupt" strategic planning objectives. A good example of this is the Rouse Hill Development Area (RHDA) on Sydney's northwestern periphery.[1] In response to an approach by a consortium of owners of land, who offered to pay for the provision of water supply, drainage and sewage systems, the NSW government agreed, in the late 1980s, to the urbanization of the land well ahead of what would have been achievable with traditional public-sector infrastructure provision. In an area of 9,400 hectares, the locality will eventually be able to accommodate approximately 250,000 persons in around 70,000 dwelling units.

The effect of the consortium taking responsibility for front-end financing and construction of hydraulic infrastructure has been the advancement of development a number of years ahead of the capability of other infrastructure providers to obtain adequate funding for other necessary infrastructure through "section 94" contributions (EPAA),[2] loan funds or through the normal state budgetary process. The approach adopted by the consortium was possible due to their substantial land holdings that will enjoy substantial increases in value.

Stage 1 of the RHDA development approximately coincides with the major land holdings of consortium members and is now fully serviced and available for development. Stage 1 is, however, a set of spatially fragmented land holdings and this has significant implications for the provision of human services infrastructure. Primary schools and community facilities will, for example, need to be provided in each of the separate areas in the Stage or else will not be provided at all in some areas, at significant additional cost to the providers and/or users. The problem of fragmentation also applies to regional-level services. The RHDA is envisaged as a self-contained area but is remote from existing centers of service provision. Yet it will be many years before demand thresholds required to provide regional services within RHDA will be achieved.

A related example of how privatized infrastructure provision has corrupted broader planning objectives is the construction of the F2 urban freeway that serves the north west sector. One of the reasons that this sector was favored for major urban development was the existence of a railway line into the area, although major upgrading was required. The NSW Auditor General examined the F2 freeway arrangements between the state government and the Hills Motorway company and concluded that, as a result of those arrangements, the "optimum transport solution" for the north west sector may be delayed for up to 45 years. This is because contractual arrangements make the state liable for any loss of revenue resulting from the construction of competing transport systems, such as railway upgrading. This stricture will perpetuate the cycle of automobile dependency with the social costs it implies. In a more localized sense, it may be noted that the RHDA is itself remote from the existing railway line and this will further encourage automobile dependence.

Iı. Cost recovery pricing of urban infrastructure

The trend to cost recovery pricing for urban infrastructure reflects not just the financial pressures on governments noted above but also recognition, since the early 1980s, of the extent to which urban infrastructure is under-priced (Commonwealth Industry Commission 1993). Whatever its efficiency merits, this trend raises important equity issues since, because of the city's particular socio-spatial structure (referred to above), lower income groups tend to be disproportionately affected. A counter argument is that not only does appropriate pricing ensure that providers can meet demand, but cost recovery pricing also extends to "externality" pricing which is the lynch pin of ecologically sustainable cities. Social justice interests may concede environmentalist viewpoints yet reject effective means to maintain ecological sustainability. The case of leaded versus unleaded petrol is illustrative. To encourage owners to rapidly retire the stock of cars which burn leaded petrol would require a much larger differential in petrol prices than exists now. But it is older cars that burn leaded petrol and poorer people predominantly own these. Another example concerns tolls on urban freeways in Sydney. Equity, it is claimed, demands that tolls be removed since it is longer-distance commuters from especially the outer western and southwestern suburbs of Sydney who use them most. Such people are assumed to be poorer than average. They are also more car dependent due to lack of public transport that in turn reflects the poor economics of low residential densities. There is also the issue of inter-generational equity, one of the principles of ecologically sustainable development, because those who live in the established parts of the city have available for their use roads for which they do not have to pay (at least directly). The dilemma is that road pricing to reflect environmental damage is the only logical way to reduce behavior deleterious to the environment.

In principle such equity impacts need not be unmanageable. The Interim Report of the Economic Planning and Advisory Council's *Task Force on Private Infrastructure* (May 1995) discusses the distributional impacts of user pays and, by extension, externality pricing. There are indirect and direct means to compensate those least able to absorb increased costs of living resulting from measures to protect the environment.[3] Whether compensation is offered in practice is altogether another matter.

III. Exercise of state power over local government

Local government is not provided for under the Australian constitution but rather is a creature of state legislation. It is thus always capable of being overridden by state government if it behaves in a manner inconsistent with state managerial and entrepreneurial objectives. The key piece of legislation through which the NSW government pursues its managerialist objectives in relation to Sydney is the Environmental Planning and Assessment Act (EPAA). The principles of this Act include division of planning powers between state and local government (s.5b) and direct citizen participation in decision-making (s.5c). The EPAA does, however, enable exclusion of local government and citizens from planning decisions under certain circumstances (Farrier 1993, 28-29). Provisions in the EPAA to override local government, and the use of special legislation to override the EPAA itself, have been used since the EPAA was enacted in 1980. The propensity of state governments to exercise those options has accelerated in response to managerial and entrepreneurial imperatives.

The NSW government has, for example, sought to promote higher residential densities in Sydney since the early 1980s. The primary reason is to reduce the need to provide new urban infrastructure due to financial pressures deriving from globalization. The political problem in promoting higher residential densities is that, whilst they may beneficial at the level of the metropolitan region, they do not obviously benefit the residents of particular parts of the city. The unwillingness of local government to support the state position has produced continuing conflict. As a result, the state has used its powers under the EPAA to override local decision-making authority in relation to residential densities.

There are several recent instances where globally driven, state-promulgated objectives of urban governance have been used as justifications for neutralizing local government and precluding citizen participation in the making of planning decisions. Typically the state interest has derived from its entrepreneurial agenda. The redevelopment of Darling Harbour in the late 1980s is a case in point. This was a government-owned railway and port facility on the western edge of Sydney's central business district. Technological change in freight handling (the shift to containerization and large ships) had made the site redundant by the late 1970s. The then state government perceived that there was a major opportunity to construct a waterside recreational and shopping complex, modeled on Baltimore's much mimicked inner harbor project, as a device for encouraging economic development through tourism. The aim was also to catalyze redevelopment of the adjacent Pyrmont-Ultimo district—a rundown inner city residential area and industrial zone. To eliminate the possibility of local 'interference' the state government passed the Darling Harbour Authority Act that created a development agency excluding local influence (Farrier 1993, 43). It is also pertinent to note that the redevelopment was "fast tracked" to counter the perceived competitive advantage Brisbane (Queensland's capital) would derive from holding the 1988 Trade Expo.

Another notable and recent example of the trend concerns the leasing to Fox Studios of Sydney's historic inner city Showground at Moore Park (located just to the south east of the CBD). The positive aspect to this case is that Fox Studios was thereby attracted to establish a major film production facility in Sydney (against competition from Melbourne). As well as providing employment and short term investment benefits, the studios will hopefully contribute to the development of the cultural economy of Sydney. The negative aspects of the case relate to the financial deal between Fox and the state government, the elimination of public access to land originally designated for that purpose, and the exclusion of public input to the site's planning. Williams (1997) provides an excellent analysis of this case. In relation to the general trend these cases exemplify, Farrier (1993, 44) argues that, "Although it is quite clear that the State Government, acting through the legislature, is legally entitled to act as it did in these cases, some people would dispute its moral right to do so. Adopting this sort of approach leaves the government open to accusations of riding roughshod over the environmental planning legislation."

The Rise of Entrepreneurialism

Economic globalization has thus directly and indirectly influenced Sydney's managerialist governance. But whilst entrepreneurialism has become interrelated with managerialism through the production of the city's built environment, it also has a "life of its own." The NSW Department of

State and Regional Development is the official entrepreneurial arm of government and is charged with promoting the state as an investment site and with doing deals with investors. State-driven entrepreneurialism gives rise to Australian states competing for investment and consumption flows. Whilst not unique to Australia, competition is especially pronounced here because of the federal system of government. The Australian government's Industry Commission (1997) being highly critical of the contemporary phase has generally regarded competition as inefficient from a national economic perspective. An implication for urban managerialism is that funds that might otherwise be available for provision and maintenance of urban infrastructure are diverted to subsidies induced by inter-state competition. Currently in Sydney there is some evidence of diversion of funds to support the 2000 Olympics, the biggest of global marketing opportunities.

It is not, however, just the official arms of elected government that drive entrepreneurial governance. Increasingly, urban growth coalitions are emerging. Hall and Hubbard (1996) define these as consisting of loose or informal partnerships of a multiplicity of interest groups that function together in order to make and carry out governing decisions. "Members" include property interest, rentiers, utility groups, universities, business groups, trade unions, and the media. Formed in late 1997, the Committee for Sydney, modeled on the Committee for London (Newman and Thornley 1997), is rooted in the conviction of its prime mover, prominent Sydney lawyer and civic entrepreneur, Mr. Rod McGeoch (a key player in winning the Olympics for Sydney), that Sydney is simply not doing enough to promote itself. In the *Sydney Morning Herald* of 23 August 1996, McGeoch was reported as saying, "My sense of Sydney at the moment is that, as a result of our natural advantages and our successes such as winning the Olympics, a complacency is afoot which cities such as Melbourne are taking advantage of to reassert their own position and which, beyond 2000, we may have cause to regret." In its manifesto published in 1998, the Committee for Sydney cautioned that "if we are not careful, Sydney could be outsmarted by other cities [and] we have to think smarter, work harder and plan better if we are to build a viable future for our city in an intensely and increasingly competitive regional and world economy."

Hall and Hubbard (1996) point out that coalitions are nearly always formed around the idea of achieving visible, concrete policy results within a limited time span and the ephemeral nature of many coalitions tends to result in a piecemeal approach to urban development that lacks strategic foresight or long-term planning. Against this is the shift of the National Roads and Motorists Association (NRMA) from being purely an advocate of motorists interests to a serious concern about air pollution and the need for major investment in public transport. The NRMA's recent *Clean Air* 2000 strategy sets out a quite detailed strategic plan for Sydney. Although in no way an arm of government, the Association is clearly doing the government's job and actually has senior bureaucrats and government ministers on its team. Mr. Rod McGeoch chaired the taskforce that prepared the strategy.

Welfare Outcomes

What have not so far been emphasized in the paper are the forms of resistance that have arisen around the globally driven shifts in urban management practices and the rise of entrepreneurialism. To do justice to this subject would extend the present paper beyond reasonable bounds, but its importance is undoubted and some very general points can be made by way of conclusion. The matters of equity outcomes of cost recovery pricing, and the undermining of strategic land-use planning that may arise from privatized infrastructure provision, have been referred to. So too have local resistances to state-driven policies to promote higher residential densities been mentioned. Opportunity costs associated with inter-state competition, although this has not been a matter of much public debate, is another significant by-product of entrepreneurialism. It should also be noted that there has been major community resistance to expanded capacity at Kingsford Smith Airport and to the proposed construction of a new airport at Badgery's Creek in Sydney's west, to intraurban freeway development generally, and the handing over of the former Sydney Showground at Moore Park to Fox Studios. An important issue too is the apparent impact of spending on the Olympics on service provision generally but especially in the new growth areas in outer Sydney. The east-west welfare divide—the essence of Sydney's social geography—is thus arguably being exacerbated (Murphy and Watson 1994). Some argue too that the policies to increase residential densities referred to above —are also deepening the socio-spatial gulf in the city (Troy 1996). Whatever the glib rhetoric of the state government and civic boosters, there are some major questions as to who benefits from the current fashion for city marketing.

Notes

[1] This section of the paper is based on D. Tow (1995)

[2] Under section 94 of the NSW Environmental Planning and Assessment Act, local government councils may levy charges on developers to defray the costs of local government services that may be required as a result of a development. For example, a housing subdivision, when occupied, may generate demand for a local library. The cost of meeting this demand may be levied against the developer.

[3] Two categories of indirect means of compensation may be identified. First, as higher levels of resource costs for infrastructure provision are recovered, governments may be able to decrease taxes or to increase spending elsewhere. A second option arises when reductions in charges for business users (e.g. of water), consequent upon the removal of cross subsidies, may be partly passed on to consumers in the form of lower prices.

Three direct means of compensation may be deployed by governments when people are adversely affected by externality pricing, and cost recovery pricing generally. First, direct payments may be made to individuals designated through means testing. Second, payments, equal to the differences between the full costs of service provision and the subsidized price which governments deem appropriate for designated groups, may be made to service providers. A third compensatory option is for public sector providers to reduce the required rate of return on their assets, thereby reducing government dividend requirements.

References

Australian Bureau of Statistics. 1998. *Sydney: a social atlas.* Canberra: AGPS.

Commonwealth Grants Commission. 1995. *Reports on Research in Progress, 1995.* Volume 1. Canberra: AGPS.

Commonwealth Grants Commission. 1993. *Report on General Grant Relativities 1993, Volume II—Methods, Assessments and Analysis.* Canberra: AGPS.

Commonwealth Industry Commission. 1997. *State, territory and local government assistance to industry.* Canberra: AGPS.

Commonwealth Industry Commission. 1993. *Taxation and financial policy impacts on urban settlement.* Draft Report, Vol. 1. Canberra: AGPS.

Commonwealth of Australia. 1996. *State of the environment report.* Canberra: AGPS.

Economic Planning and Advisory Council. 1995. *Private Infrastructure Task Force: Interim Report.* Canberra: AGPS.

Farrier, D. 1993. *The environmental law handbook: planning and land use in New South Wales.* Sydney: Redfern Legal Centre Publishing.

Hall, T. and P. Hubbard. 1996. The entrepreneurial city: new urban politics, new urban geographies? *Progress in Human Geography.* 20, 2: 153-174.

Harding, A. 1994. Urban regimes and growth machines: towards a cross-national research agenda. *Urban Affairs Quarterly.* 29, 3: 356-382.

Harvey, D. 1989. Urban places in the global village: reflections on the urban condition in late twentieth century capitalism. *World cities and the future of metropoles.* Edited by L. Mazza. Electra, XVII Triennale. 21-32.

Kirwan, R. 1990. Infrastructure finance: aims, attitudes and approaches. *Urban Policy and Research.* 8: 185-93.

Murphy, P. and S. Watson. 1997. *Surface city: Sydney at the millennium.* Sydney: Pluto Press.

Murphy, P. and S. Watson. 1994. Social polarisation and Australian cities. *International Journal of Urban and Regional Research.* 18: 573-590.

National Roads and Motorists Association. 1997. *Clean air 2000: strategic action plan, 1997-2000.* Sydney.

New South Wales Department of State and Regional Development. 1997. *Sydney Investment Profile.* Sydney.

New South Wales, Department of Urban Affairs and Planning. 1997. A *framework for growth and change: the review of strategic planning.* Sydney.

New South Wales Government. 1997. *Tourism Strategy for Sydney.* Sydney.

New South Wales Government. 1991. *Sydney's future: a discussion paper on planning the greater metropolitan region.* Sydney.

New South Wales, Independent Pricing and Regulatory Tribunal. 1996. *Inquiry into the Pricing of Public Passenger Transport Services.* Sydney.

New South Wales, Local Government Grants Commission. 1995. *Annual Report 1994/95.* Sydney.

Newman, P. and A Thornley. 1997. Fragmentation and centralisation in the governance of London: influencing the urban policy and planning agenda. *Urban Studies.* 34, 7: 967-988.

Sassen, S. 1991. *The global city.* Princeton: Princeton University Press.

Tow, D. 1995. *The effectiveness of metropolitan planning for the Sydney region.* Unpublished Policy Paper, Master of Public Policy, University of Sydney.

Troy, P.N. 1996. *The perils of urban consolidation.* Sydney: Federation Press.

Sandercock, L. 1998. *Towards metropolis: planning for multicultural cities.* Chichester: John Wiley.

Vipond, J. 1985. Unemployment—a current issue of intra-urban inequalities. *Living in cities.* Edited by I.H. Burnley and J. Forrest. Sydney: Allen and Unwin. 116-127.

Williams, P. 1997. Out-foxing the people? Recent state involvement in the planning system. *Urban Policy and Research.* 15, 2: 129-136.

WON BAE KIM

National Competitiveness and Governance of Seoul, Korea

E ven before the current financial crisis hit the Korean economy, there had been numerous warnings about its failing competitiveness. Coined as the four highs, the Korean economy was suffering, it was said, from high interest rates, high wages, high land prices, and high circulation costs. In other words, it was characterized by high costs and low efficiency. The government sector, in particular, was criticized for its rigidity and inefficiency. Would this mean an end to the state-led development model of Asia? Some argued that the traditional top-down approach was no longer effective in the changed environment of the global economy. The state, which had once played a critical role in shaping the path of economic development in Korea, was now regarded as an obstacle. Whether one subscribes to this view or not, there is a widening consensus in Korea that the role of state must be redefined in line with the changed circumstances of globalization and the pluralization of Korean society.

In government circles, the foremost role of the state at the moment is perceived to be that of restoring the competitive advantage of the economy.[1] An economy-wide reform is needed, involving significant de-regulation. Obviously, the direction taken by the government places a heavy emphasis on the "invisible hand" of the market. Among some radical reformers, deregulation is believed to be the solution for all the ills created by government intervention in the past.

Amidst these ongoing efforts to restructure the Korean economy, debates have been intensified about the competitiveness of cities and city-regions. Acknowledging that city-regions are the real battleground between nations in economic war, concerned policy-makers, scholars, and entrepreneurs have suggested various prescriptions to enhance the international competitiveness of city-regions (Kim et al. 1997; Korea Economic Research Institute 1995). One of them is directly related to land use and planning. Over-regulation and over-planning are criticized for their negative effects on international competitiveness. For example, high land prices are attributed to the central government's policy failure, including the tight land supply policy imposed by various planning schemes such as the greenbelt policy, which arbitrarily took out a large chunk of land from urban development. Either the complete elimination of regulations governing land use or at least a significant reduction of them, is urged by both the private sector and local governments in order to raise the international competitiveness of cities (Lee 1998). The private sector argues that deregulation will help firms to use land more efficiently, thus restoring their competitiveness. Local governments, which feel that local economic development is a solution to the national economic crisis, demand that land use regulation and planning rights should be given to them rather than left in the hands of the central government. Citizens and citizen groups are no mere spectators in this game. Residents who have been affected by various government land-related policies are demanding that their property rights be restored to them, while citizens, demanding better environmental quality, resist unwanted facilities coming into their neighborhoods.

Planners and policy-makers, on the other hand, clearly recognize the regional nature of urban problems, even including the competitiveness argument. Seoul's transportation problem, for example, is intricately linked to commuting from cities outside of Seoul. So are air pollution, water pollution, waste collection, and housing. The central government, although acknowledging the need to decentralize its power to local governments and the private sector, does not believe that the time is ripe to give up its planning and other controls over the use of land. Without its ability to control, the central government believes that major city-regions, such as Seoul, cannot be effectively governed. On the other hand, local governments claim that local autonomy backed by sufficient fiscal resources and planning powers would be a better solution with a view to maintaining their edge in global competition. What kind of governance arrangement will be best for Korea's cities remains to be seen.

The high primacy of the capital region in Korea occupies a central position in all of these debates. My discussion will therefore be focused on the capital region and the issues surrounding its management. In particular, land-use policies and regulations will be taken as examples for an in-depth discussion. While describing the role of various actors with respect to land use, I will try to address some of the issues concerning governance, especially those related to the competitiveness and sustainability of city-regions. The paper concludes with a number of suggestions for improving the current governance arrangements of large city-regions in Korea.

The Capital Region Policy:
The Heavy-handed Approach of Central Government
Korea's rapid urban-based industrialization over the past thirty years has posed enormous problems of congestion, pollution, and unbalanced regional development. The central government started to pay attention to these serious problems since the mid-1960s, with the Seoul metropolitan area as the principal focus for this effort. Numerous policies, plans, and laws have been designed to combat population and industrial concentration in the area. The first policy phase, from the mid-1960s to the mid-1970s, concentrated on the objective of containing the Seoul's continued growth. This containment policy, however, was not followed by detailed prescriptions and failed to bring significant results (Park 1995; KRIHS 1997).

The second policy phase, lasting from the mid-1970s to the mid-1980s, reinforced the preceding containment policy. Administrative measures to regulate manufacturing firms and educational institutions were introduced and the greenbelt policy was announced. The third policy phase, which occurred from the mid-1980s to the mid-1990s, introduced a more comprehensive law and management plan. The Capital Region Management Law was enacted in 1984, and the boundary of the Capital Region was officially defined to include the cities of Seoul and Inchon as well as Kyonggi province. The first Capital Region Management Plan (CRMP) was prepared to ensure a more efficient use of land, a desirable distribution of industries and population, and the efficient and equitable provision of infrastructure. The fourth policy phase lasted from the mid-1990s to the present, and a new set of policies has been sketched out for the period from 1997 to 2011. There has been a marked shift in policy emphasis between the earlier and latter two phases. Population dispersal away from Seoul was the primary objective of the early years, while population deconcentration within the Capital Region came to be emphasized in the third phase. In addition to supporting regional and intra-regional equity, the fourth phase placed an emphasis on developing and enhancing the more international functions of the Capital Region (Park 1995; KRIHS 1997).

In all these efforts, the central government played a dominant role. In the 1970s, the Presidential House supported both population deconcentration from Seoul and the greenbelt policy. However, it was the Ministry of Construction (changed later into the Ministry of Construction and Transportation) which followed up these policy initiatives. Understandably, in the strong centralized power structure of Korea, lower level governments and the civil society had no place in policymaking whatever.

The Capital Region Management Plan as a Policy Tool

In the 1970s and early 1980s, the Seoul metropolitan region was the target of the central government's dispersal policy. Accordingly, the region's boundary was defined at the time as Seoul's commuting zone. This consisted of the jurisdictions of the Seoul Special City government, parts of Kyonggi province, and the city of Inchon. But as urban problems continued to spread outward, the central government felt a need to have a more inclusive definition of the Capital Region. The officially defined area now covers the entire province of Kyonggi in addition to the jurisdictions of Seoul and Inchon.[2] As of 1995, the Capital Region had a total area of 11,718 km[2] and a population of 20.2 million. In terms of jurisdictional divisions, the region consists of one province (Kyonggi), 19 cities, and 17 counties, and the two provincial-level cities of Seoul and Inchon (KRIHS 1997).

The Capital Region is the target area of the CRMP and is subject to the Capital Region Management Law (CRML), which overrides all other laws related to development activities in this region. The Capital Region Management Plan has thus a special status and priority whenever conflicts arise between the Plan and other development plans. The Capital Region Management Review Committee is in charge of planning and policy-making. Chaired by the Prime Minister, it includes the ministers of related ministries in the central government as well as the governor of Kyonggi and the mayors of Seoul and Inchon. However, both the governor and mayors are a recent addition to the Committee, which used to include only representatives of the central government.

The long-term Capital Region Management Plan is prepared at the central government level (led by the Ministry of Construction and Transportation) and deals with the basic directions and guidelines for the capital region concerning the distribution of population and industrial activities, readjustment by zone, and region-wide facilities. Its detailed planning, however, is done at two levels. Provincial and local governments are required to make a comprehensive implementation plan, while related central government agencies have to propose detailed implementation plans for the items in their purview.[3]

The major tools of the Plan are laws and decrees regulating the development of activities inducing population dispersal. In the First Capital Region Management Plan (1984-1996), the implementation of the plan was mainly dependent on direct regulations (including the greenbelt) and assigning various types of development deemed appropriate to each of the five zones.[4] However, in the Second Plan, the reliance on direct measures was reduced, and greater use was made of indirect economic incentives. Also, reflecting the inadequacy of five-zone division of the

Capital Region, the Second Plan reduced them to only three: a congestion relief, nature conservation, and growth management zone.

In addition to this broad zoning designation, two important policy
instruments are congestion charges and an aggregate development volume system. Congestion charges are levied on those development activities that are likely to induce population concentration within the congestion relief zone (this measure is applied only to the city of Seoul at
the moment even though Inchon and some part of Kyonggi province are
included within it). Business offices, department stores, and public facilities above a certain size are also subject to the congestion charge,
usually ten percent of total construction costs.

The aggregate volume system is designed to control the growth of the
Capital Region. With a given aggregate volume of construction, individual
development activities are allowed for. Two sorts of activity are subject to
this system: factories and colleges. The Ministry of Construction and Transportation sets the total development volume of factories for each year
along with management guidelines. And the Ministry allocates quotas
for each city and county, taking local circumstances into consideration.
Then, within these quotas, the heads of local governments screen appli-
cations for factory construction. With suggestions from the governor and
mayors, the Capital Region Management Review Committee decides the
aggregate volume in the first quarter of the year.

The construction of new colleges and college expansions is, in principle, discouraged within the Capital Region, although the construction of
vocational colleges and mini-colleges with less than fifty students is
allowed (except in Seoul). The Capital Region Management Law also regu-
lates large-scale development projects. For each such project, the heads
of local and/or provincial administrative organizations must obtain
approval from the Minister of Construction and Transportation.

Pressure for Deregulation and Central Government Responses
The Capital Region Management Plan has had considerable effect in shaping the overall land use pattern. Out of the total region of 11,718 km^2,
54.9 percent are set aside for forests and fields, 26.8 percent for agriculture,
and only 8.8 percent for urban uses. Such a low share of urban land use
suggests a situation of tight land supply, driving prices upward. The more
important problem, however, is the spatial distribution of this land in
relation to activities. Currently, population and industrial activities are
over-concentrated in the *congestion relief zone*, which accounts for only 18
percent of the area but for 87 percent of the population and 78 percent of
all factories (KRIHS 1997). On the other hand, the large *growth management*

zone to the north and the south accounts for only 9.8 percent of the total population, on 49.4 percent of area. To the west, the *nature conservation zone* accounts for 32.7 percent in terms of area and 3.0 percent in terms of population. In addition, the introduction of the greenbelt in and around Seoul in the early 1970s has greatly affected the land use pattern of the region. Some claim that the arbitrary designation of greenbelt has caused a leapfrogging pattern of urban sprawl (Sohn 1996). By reducing the supply of land for development, the policy is sometimes blamed for the exorbitant land price increases in the Capital Region.

As the Korean economy began experiencing a decline in its inter-national competitiveness, pressure mounted for deregulation, especially targeting the "excessive regulations" of land uses in the Capital Region. Riding this wave of deregulation and, in general, the liberalization of the Korean economy as a whole, industrialists, developers, and private sector organizations appealed to the central government for a relaxation of land-use controls. The proponents of deregulation took the national competitiveness argument as a key for cracking the government's grip on land- use planning. For example, the Federation of Korean Industries and the Korean Chamber of Commerce and Industry, siding with scholars of neo-liberal persuasion, demanded deregulation of what they considered unnecessary government intervention, including land use controls (Korea Chamber of Commerce and Industry 1997; Choe 1996; Sohn 1996). Their reasoning is that, whether one likes it or not, the Capital Region is the only region in Korea able to compete with other major city-regions in in the world. Impairing its competitiveness through an excess of regulations and restrictions would be detrimental to the stable growth of the Korean economy. Even though urban problems such as traffic congestion and environmental pollution have to be ameliorated, these problems should be dealt with through various market-conforming measures, such as pollution charges and congestion fees.[5] Blanket land-use restrictions by laws and administrative decrees by the government are deemed unnecessary.

They further argued that more advanced service functions, high-tech industries, universities, and research institutions are needed to enhance the international competitiveness of the Region. Large office buildings that can accommodate multinational corporations' regional headquar-ters should be allowed to be built without penalty. Restrictions on fac-tory construction within the Capital Region are no longer effective, be-cause firms in this "borderless age" can move out of the country, and may even to the "hollowing-out" of the Capital Region. Besides, the aggregate volume control in the CRML and the Industry Distribution Law, doubly controlling factory construction in the Capital Region, should be eliminated to enhance the competitiveness of domestic firms as well as to induce foreign direct investments (Lee 1998).

It was not just the private sector which demanded the elimination of excessive land-use regulations. Local governments did as well. With the beginning of local autonomy in 1994, provincial and local governments have become increasingly interested in local economic development. Each province or city has been striving to host more firms and business activities in its own territory. Kyonggi province, the special cities of Seoul and Inchon, and smaller cities and counties within the Capital Region are no exception. Recognizing that their development is constrained by the Capital Region Management Law, provincial and local governments have begun to join the battle for renegotiating the status of their respective areas, seeking exceptions from the rules specified in the CRML. With limited fiscal independence, local governments have not been making direct criticisms against the central government but have been working in various ways to maneuver themselves out of the tight regulations imposed by the central government. For example, Kyonggi province has submitted proposals to eliminate the aggregate volume control system applying to factory construction (*Chosun Ilbo*, 5 November 1996). It argued that those factories which had already obtained a factory establishment permit, should also be given a permit to build. At the same time, existing factories classified as high-tech industries should be allowed to expand on- or off-site. The city of Inchon, the whole area of which was designated as congestion relief zone, has appealed to the central government and has succeeded in reclassifying part of its territory into a growth management zone.[6]

Reluctantly accepting the claim that land-use regulations had reduced the supply of land, the central government revised the National Land Use and Management Law in 1994, by which a large tract of rural land (called the "semi-agricultural zone") was designated as a new source of land for urban expansion. The major beneficiary of this law will be the Capital Region.

According to the revision, any buildings except for pollution-generating facilities, large facilities with a site requirement larger than 30,000 square meters, and certain dining and lodging facilities are allowed in this "semi-agricultural zone." Because development activities in the semi-agricultural zone are not subject to the Urban Planning Law they are only loosely controlled. As was to be expected, chaotic development followed the introduction of the new classification, and soon there were calls for tighter regulation. One suggestion was to merge the semi-agricultural zone with the urban zone to make it conform to Urban Planning Law for a more orderly development.

Another notable feature of the 1994 Revised National Land Use and Management Law is the stimulation of the private sector in land development. Public-private partnerships and/or the utilization of the "third," non-government sector were strongly recommended. The private sector, like the public, is now allowed to use "eminent domain" for land acquisition[7] and has also been given the power to develop industrial estates, a power which heretofore had been reserved to the the government.

The Ministry of Construction and Transportation, representing the central government, has also acknowledged the need for changes in the CRMP. It accepted the criticisms that the Capital Region Policy is too rigid and out of tune with changed circumstances, and revised the Capital Region Management Law. These changes were reflected in the Second Capital Region Management Plan (KRIHS 1997). Outright restrictions on certain development activities have been changed to indirect measures, such as congestion charges, in order to accommodate increasing space demand for advanced business services, and information and research functions. High-tech industries are now allowed to freely locate in the Capital Region, but factories considered undesirable (e.g., polluting industries and simple assembly factories) continue to be discouraged.[8]

While pro-market (anti-regulation) voices are gathering force among business circles, local governments within the Capital Region, sympathetic policy-makers and government officials in the central Ministries in charge of economic affairs (especially the Ministry of Industry and Resources), as well as a pro-planning camp that includes the Ministry of Construction and Transportation, environmentalists, and some citizen groups strongly endorse some form of regulation for the Capital Region's future growth (Park 1996). Their reasoning is based on arguments defending the "quality of life" and "balanced regional development." The pro-planning camp regards the criticisms from the anti-regulationists as representing primarily the interests of large corporations and a few localities. They worry that the relaxation of regulations in the revised Capital Region Management Law may result in a "disorderly" development detrimental to the environment (KRIHS 1997; Kwon 1998).

Greenbelt Policy Under Pressure

The greenbelt policy has been in dispute since its implementation in 1971. The new administration, which in its election platform had promised a readjustment of the policy, is now seriously considering the issue. Unlike the CRML, which is concerned primarily with new development activities related to manufacturing, business, and universities, greenbelt policy is seen to impinge directly on citizens' property rights. It is, therefore, essentially a dispute between the state, on the one hand, and the land-owners and residents affected by the policy. There have been constant appeals and complaints about the side effects of the greenbelt restrictions. Some scholars have criticized it as a major policy failure, because the greenbelt reduced land supply and encouraged a leap-frogging pattern of urban developments beyond the belt (Sohn 1993). As a matter of fact, the details of the policy have been revised more than 40 times since 1977. Especially around election times and under pressure from politicians, the central government relaxed activity restrictions. Such *ad hoc* measures merely damaged the integrity of the greenbelt without bringing real benefits to residents. It is a great irony that it was precisely the public sector that was the major culprit in inflicting damage (Kwon 1998).

Recognizing the fundamental importance of property rights, the new administration is considering various ways to compensate for the loss of benefits by the property owners in the greenbelt area. Most citizens, while agreeing with the principle of compensation, have doubts whether there is an equitable and just way of compensation that will not jeopardize the original purpose of the policy.[9] The Ministry of Construction and Transportation has suggested three options (*Kyonghyang Shinmun*, 16 March 1998). The first is to relax activity restrictions within the greenbelt area, the second is to remove some portion from the designated greenbelt area, and the third is to free activity restrictions by area and land use categories. Although the Ministry prefers the third option, the proposed solution may not satisfy either residents or the ruling party. Both appear to favor the second option, even though this would generate problems of fairness and the appropriatness of selection criteria. One possible solution would be to relieve settlement areas of more than twenty households from greenbelt restrictions, but this would only remove a small portion from the total greenbelt area.[10] Environmental groups have already expressed their concern, however, that such a relaxation of the "sacred" greenbelt policy would induce land speculation and high-density developments. Another option which might satisfy both environmental concerns and the property rights of landowners would be for the government to purchase these land plots at a fair price. Given the present economic crisis, however, this option is unlikely to find much favor in policy circles.

Each actor involved directly or indirectly in this debate has a different position with respect policy options. How the final outcome will unfold depends on the politics among the contestants. But if the political process does not meet the following minimum conditions, disputes about the greenbelt policy will simply continue. They are: the final decision must be arrived at through an open process involving all the relevant actors, including ruling party, landowners and greenbelt residents, central government agencies, and concerned environmental groups; a consensus must be reached on appropriate principles and methods of compensation; and a comprehensive greenbelt plan must be devised for long-term management.

Competitiveness, Sustainability, and Governance of the Capital Region

International competitiveness of the Capital Region has been the catchphrase of deregulation proponents. Their logic is straightforward. Numerous regulations on land use in the Capital Region have reduced the supply of land and resulted in steep increases in the price of land. Inceased prices and rents, in turn, have increased the production costs and led to a decline in the productivity of firms. Although no one disputes this fact, when proposed as a cause for the declining competitiveness of the Capital Region and projected as a way to increase its economic vitality, the argument is faulty.

First of all, Korea's falling productivity was a result of not just high land prices but, more importantly, of high wages and capital costs. Secondly, a firm's competitiveness is not equivalent to a city's competitiveness. The international competitiveness of a city depends on a whole series of factors, including its process of governance, the social and economic infrastructure, the quality of its human capital, the quality of its natural environment, its business environment, and the capacity of financial institutions (Kim 1997; Friedmann 1998). Therefore, even if high land prices are accepted as a cause for the falling competitiveness of the Capital Region, there is no guarantee that increased land supply, and hence lower land rents, will improve the region's competitiveness overall. If land use deregulation causes irreparable damage to the environment, a region's competitiveness will surely decline in the long run. Neoclassical economic solutions, such as congestion pricing and pollution charges for urban externalities, are theoretically good, but they also incur heavy enforcement costs. Moreover, on the basis of a private cost calculus, they would leave out the social costs of externalities.

A neo-liberal view on a region's competitiveness inevitably involves a contradictory relationship between competitiveness and sustainability. But in the long run, a socially and environmentally sustainable region is not incompatible with a productive one. As Korea's Capital Region becomes primarily a knowledge-based economy, social and environmental capital acquire greater importance in developing a liveable, productive region (Friedmann 1998).

Inasmuch as a region's economic performance is intertwined with the quality of its life, governance arrangements are becoming more important (OECD 1998). A region's ability to govern itself effectively as well as efficiently is essential to its economic competitiveness and sustainability. Although there is no direct relationship between governance and economic performance, city-regions in many parts of the world must rethink their forms of governance in a context where the fortunes of nation states are becoming increasingly dependent on their major cities (Friedmann 1998; OECD 1998).

With its strong tradition of centralism, Korea's major urban development and land-use decisions have been made by the central government. Because of its paramount importance in the national economy, the Capital Region—as is the case of many other primate cities of Asia (McGee 1995)—has been given special status and has been governed by special laws (and plans). Local governments, however, complain about the excessive concentration of power in the hands of the central government. Such centralization appears contradictory with the widely used rhetoric of decentralization. Even when admiting that local governments are not yet in a position to make sensible plans, policy-making at the central level should bring local government into the planning process. The monopoly of planning power at the central level has resulted in various problems with respect to governance, particularly in terms of criteria such as transparency, inclusiveness, efficiency, and effectiveness.

Although the transparency issue has been somewhat mitigated in recent years, major decisions regarding land use and infrastructure in the past were made by central government without a set of general principles and clearly understood procedures. The arbitrary designation of the greenbelt is a prime example of a closed decision making process and has been frequently criticized for its arbitrariness.

In regional development as well as urban planning, local government does not have independent power to make plans. Although local units are substantially involved in the implementation of planning, they do so by delegation from the central government. Even in the restricted area of urban planning and land use, where local units have better knowledge and understanding, planning powers largely remain with the central government. Local units act merely as the agents of the central government in their implementation.

Under these conditions, it is only very recently that the central government has tried to solicit ideas from provincial and local governments for national-level planning. Until then, little consideration had been given to either the private sector or civil society. Individual citizens and citizen groups, who have recently stood against government decisions affecting their life, have begun to make some impact on this process. However, their influence is for the most part limited to small facility location decisions, such as waste fills, crematories, etc. Their participation is desired primarily at the community level but not yet at the regional level.

With respect to the Capital Region Management Policy, there is a widespread perception that the policy has not achieved the goals of population and industrial deconcentration (Lee 1998). Rather, because of its too ambitious goals and certain structural defects, it has produced negative side effects. Unregistered factories are a good example. Across the Capital Region, small-scale factories which could not afford to pay high land costs and emission charges have mushroomed. For a variety of reasons, these factories had to be given legal recognition with only promises of future improvement (Hwang 1996).

Despite negative scores on criteria of transparency and inclusiveness, the regional governance system heavily controlled by the central government has some merits. It is efficient in terms of decision making and suitable for serving the larger collective interest. For example, most newspapers and citizen associations endorse the greenbelt policy even though they criticize the tendency of the central government promising policy change to win votes. Also supported are the purposes of the Capital Region Management Policy to deconcentrate population and industry. If left to lower levels of government, region-wide problems such as the greenbelt, transportation, water supply, and environmental conservation are unlikely to be easily and consistently managed.

Challenges in Delivering Systems of Governance of Korea's Capital Region

Two important problems facing the governance of Korea's Capital Region are inclusiveness and collaboration (Kim et al. 1995). Many concerned scholars, planners, and administrators have recently discussed the problem of inclusiveness. Everyone agrees with the devolution of power from the central to local government and citizens. But the issue is how to share the power for a better governance of the city-region? The Korean system at the moment is close to an agent model, whereby the central government holds the effective power to make policies and local governments merely implements central decisions. A shift from this agent model to a partnership model is suggested. In order to build a partnership between the central and local government, the decentralization of power from the centre to the locality should be carried out. First of all, local government should be given the power draft plans. The current system, in which the central government has a monopoly of planning, cannot reflect regional perspectives and ideas. Deprived of this planning power, local government loses an interest in actively participating development activities.

Because of a history of centralized administration, lower level governments are in most cases not equipped with the personnel and resources to formulate plans. Therefore, local planning capacity should be greatly enhanced. One scheme being implemented at the moment is to dispatch experienced central government officials to the local level to help raise the planning capacity there. Secondly, given the weak fiscal power of most localities, new methods of tax sharing between the central and local government or giving taxation power to the locality are under discussion.

In addition to this rearrangement of centre-local power sharing, coordination and collaboration between the central and local government on plans and policies is listed as a top priority (Kim et al. 1995; Yoo et al. 1995). Cooperation with the affected local government at both provincial and city levels with respect to major policy changes or planning seems necessary to reduce potential conflicts between the central and local government. It is only very recently that the governor of Kyonggi and the mayors of Seoul and Inchon were included in the Capital Region Management Review Committee. Close consultation and collaboration between the central and local government will thus help improve the effectiveness of plan implementation.

Another aspect related to the inclusiveness as well as the effectiveness criterion is coordination between local government units. In the Capital Region, a close coordination among the provincial government of Kyonggi, the city government of Seoul and Inchon is called for. Although there is an inter-governmental consultation committee for the Capital Region (among the three upper-level local units), it has neither real decision making power nor manpower on a regular basis. To make the inter-governmental consultation committee to work, it is suggested to guarantee the participation of local representatives and to establish a permanent committee for practical tasks as a short- to medium-term measure (The Committee for Kyonggi Development in the 21st Century 1997). In the long run, the committee can be transformed into a full-blown organization with real decision making power.

However, such a less centralized, more horizontal model of governance will not be materialized in the near future. For the time being, the most likely course will be for the central government to continue playing a key role, with local government in a subsidiary role in the governance of the Capital Region. As a matter of fact, a Transportation Planning Committee has been established in 1998 to deal with region-wide transportation problems of large city-regions, including the Capital Region. As in the case of Capital Region Management Review Committee, this

Committee is headed by the Minister of Construction and Transportation and its members include several central government agencies and governors and mayors of related cities and provinces (Ministry of Construction and Transportation 1998). How effective the Committee will be remains to be seen. Similar task forces under the central government may be expected to be organized for functional areas such as water supply, refuse collection, sewage treatment, etc.

This centralized governance model with some elements of partnership is more likely than a locally-oriented governance model, such as the administrative consultation committee for large city-regions (inter-municipality governance model). Creating a metropolitan government or planning agency would be a solution as in the cases of Toronto and Vancouver (supra-municipality model) but it does not appear to have a good fit with Korea's political culture (Lefevre 1998).

Synthesizing the elements discussed above, it seems desirable to revise the Capital Region Management Law so that it will incorporate some of the issues concerning the transparency, inclusiveness, effectiveness, and efficiency of region-wide management of urban development and land use. One way to improve the current governance system would be to institutionalize local participation in the Capital Region Management Plan. By giving more power to the local level for drafting plans and project proposals, the central government can establish a partnership with upper-level local governments. The administrative consultation committee provided with real decision making power and coordination function can resolve any inconsistencies or conflicts between local-level governments. The central government, represented by the Ministry of Construction and Transportation, would suggest policy directions and targets corresponding to the principles of the CRMP. It could designate areas in broad categories, but the details of regulations and specifics would be left to the respective local governments. The Ministry could still retain the power to examine the details of plan by disaggregated area, and suggest changes whenever necessary.

Once the above arrangement (the partnership model between the central and local government) proves successful, then a more decentralized model of governance giving due recognition to citizens and the private can be developed. For example, a consultation and review committee organized by the respective local governments (Kyonggi Province, Seoul and Inchon City Government in the case of the Capital Region) with the participation of local representatives can function as an independent organization to deal with region-wide problems. The central government agencies can sit in and provide assistance in this committee and may act as a mediator when conflicts arise. Several subcommittees can be established under this committee to deal with functional areas such as transportation, environment, water supply, and so forth.

Conclusions

The Korean model of city-region governance has evolved from a centralized political system. Even though the power of the central government has recently been waning against the rise of civil society and local autonomy, it still retains substantial power in policy-making related to urban development and land uses. Given Korea's economic crisis, the erosion of the centralized system is likely to be accelerated from the globalization process and hence suggests an increasing role of transnational corporations and the business sector in general. The national competitiveness argument favored by neo-liberal economists is gaining a momentum and exerts pressure for the deregulation of perceived obstacles to economic growth. In addition, local governments and citizens increasingly challenge the central government. While realizing that their futures are not in their hands, local governments are demanding a significant decentralization of power. Increasing competition between cities and regions globally as well as domestically drives local government's interest toward local economic development without paying due considerations on the inter-connectedness of urban problems. Except for a few citizen groups, citizens in general are concerned primarily with the localized issues such as a siting of unwanted facilities and micro-scale land-use change in their neighborhood.

In this interplay of diverse groups in the urban arena, public interest as well as long-term competitiveness of city-regions are often forgotten. An emphasis on short-term competitiveness (mostly within the domain of price competition rather than non-price competition) poses a conflict between regional competitiveness and quality of life, while making the issue of governance complicated. Shaping urban growth in an orderly form and protecting urban environment are not in conflict with the long-run competitiveness of city-regions. The real issue lies in how policy decisions concerning the long-term future of city-regions are arrived. How transparent the process is, who is accountable for, how inclusive the decision making process is, whether the policy is effective or not are some of the criteria with which citizens and various interest groups can judge the policy for support or non-support.

In order to secure more public support at the regional level, the current decision making process should be more transparent and inclusive. The central government should bring in local governments in major decisions concerning the macro-structure of the Capital Region, while delegating power of detailed planning and management to the local level. Senior-level local governments such as Kyonggi province, Seoul and Inchon, on the other hand should closely consult with each other on region-wide issues and problems and develop integrated plans and policy. In addition to this horizontal cooperation, upper-level local governments should elicit and fully reflect the concerns of lower-level local governments (cities and counties) and citizens. This multi-tiered governance structure with both vertical and horizontal relationship may be ideal but its effectiveness remains doubtful because of shared decision making power. The Korean model therefore is moving slowly from the top-heavy structure, where the central government still plays a key role. An alternative foreseen in the future is a structure in which larger local units such as provinces and large cities play a leading role while the central government acts as both facilitator and moderator.

Notes

[1]   The definition of competitiveness can vary depending on the level and unit of analysis. The most widely adopted framework for national or regional level analysis is Porter's (1990) diamond model, incorporating the following four factors: factor endowment, demand condition, related and supporting industries, and firm strategy. Whichever definition of national competitiveness is used, the productivity of the Korean economy has been declining since the late 1980s, a time when the country experienced an explosion of political demands for greater freedom, economic justice, and a better quality of life.

[2]   Whether this definition of Capital Region is under-bounded or over-bounded remains an issue. But most scholars and policy-makers agree with it although there are some questions with respect to the boundary of the Region in economic terms. For example, many factories have moved down to south, Chungnam and Chungbuk provinces, and west to Kangwon province, resulting in commuting of some managers and employees between these factories and their homes in Seoul and Kyonggi. Even though those areas outside of the official definition of the Capital Region have close economic linkages with Seoul, they are difficult to include because the difficulties in data collection system, which is based on administrative boundaries (Kwon 1998).

[3]   Specifically, the Plan covers the following major areas: the objectives and basic direction for the capital region readjustment, the distribution of population and industrial activities and items concerning readjustment for each zone, items concerning the management of

facilities or development projects inducing population concentration, the renovation of region-wide infrastructure such as transportation, water, and sewerage, items concerning environmental conservation, items concerning support for the capital region management, and items concerning the implementation and administration of the CRMP.

[4] The First Capital Region Management Plan (1984-1996) divided the Region into five zones: relocation promotion zone, limited development zone, reserved development zone, growth inducement zone, and nature conservation zone.

[5] The Korean Chamber of Commerce and Industry (1997) suggests an elimination of all the regulations stifling the development of the Capital Region, except for those related to environment.

[6] The area around the new international airport was changed from congestion relief zone to growth management zone. Therefore, universities and high-tech industry factories can be built in this area (*Chosun Ilbo*, 11 February 1998).

[7] It is however, limited to 10 percent of total development area.

[8] On this point, however, the debate has been going between the Ministry of Construction and Transportation and the Korean Federation of Enterprises. The Ministry considers electronic assembly plants as conventional production function, while the Federation regards them high-tech industry.

[9] The greenbelt policy has two objectives: to preserve green area around the city and to prevent urban sprawl.

[10] These settlement areas occupy 215.8 km^2 out of 5,397 km^2 designated as greenbelt across the country.

References

Choe, S.C. 1996. The basic direction and strategy of the capital region in correspondence with globalization and localization. *Environmental Studies*. June 1996, 1-16. In Korean.

The Committee for Kyonggi Development in the 21st Century 1997, *Kyonggi 2020: Vision and Strategy*. Suwon, Kyonggi.

Friedmann, J. 1998. Rethinking Urban Competition and Sustainability in East Asia. Key-note address, Seoul Metropolitan Fora, Sustainable Urban Competitiveness: Rethinking East Asian Cities, 27-28 May 1998.

Healy, P. et al. 1995. Introduction: the city-crisis, change and invention. *Managing Cities: The New Urban Context*. Edited by P. Healy et al. Chichester: John Wiley & Sons.

Hwang, M.I. 1995, The status of unregistered factories and improvement measures. *Planning Information Bulletin*. June 1995, 34-41. In Korean.

Kim, Y.W., S.W. Kim, K.H. Ji, and M.S. Cha. 1995. A *Study on the Redistribution of Administrative Functions between Central and Local Governments in National Physical Plan.* Anyang: KRIHS. In Korean.

Kim, W.B., Y.S. Kwon and Y.W. Lee. 1997. *Strategies for Enhancing Local Competitiveness of Large Cities.* Anyang: KRIHS. In Korean.

Korea Chamber of Commerce and Industry. 1997a. Policy news. *Industrial Location News Letter,* October 1997, 12-16. In Korean.

Korea Chamber of Commerce and Industry. 1997b. Survey report. *Industrial Location News Letter,* September 1997, 12-16. In Korean.

Korea Economic Research Institute. 1995. *Entrepreneurial Local Management for Enhancing Local Competitiveness.* Seoul: KERI.

KRIHS (Korea Research Institute for Human Settlements). 1997. *The capital Region Management Plan* (1997-2011). Anyang: KRIHS. In Korean.

The Ministry of Construction and Transportation. 1998. Laws concerning Region-wide Transportation Management In Large City-Regions.

Kwon, Y.W. 1998. *Capital Region Study.* Seoul: Hanul Academy. In Korean.

Park, S.W. 1996. Misunderstanding and egoism with respect to the new capital region policy. *Nara Kyongje.* June 1996, 109-111. In Korean.

Lee, B.S. 1998. Land Use Regulations and Efficiency of Seoul's Economy. Paper presented at the Seoul Metropolitan Fora 1998, Sustainable Urban Competitiveness: Rethinking East Asian Cities, 27-28 May 1998. Seoul, Korea.

Lefevre, C. 1998. Metropolitan government and governance in Western countries: a critical review. *International Journal of Urban and Regional Research.* 22: 9-25.

McGee, T. 1995. Metrofitting the emerging mega-urban regions of ASEAN: an overview. *The Mega-Urban Regions of Southeast Asia.* Edited by T. McGee and I. Robinson. Vancouver: University of British Columbia Press, 3-26.

OECD (Organization for Economic Cooperation and Development). 1998. Better governance for more competitive and liveable cities. Seminar draft report. Paris: Territorial Development Service.

Park, S.Y. 1995. A mega-city and its management. *Globalization and Regional Development. Korea Research Institute for Human Settlements.* Edited by G. Lee and Y.W. Kim. Anyang: KRIHS.

Porter, M.E. 1990. *The Competitive Advantage of Nations.* New York: The Free Press.

Sohn, J.Y. 1996. The capital region policy must be changed. *Nara Kyongje* May 1996, 92-95. In Korean.

Sohn, J.Y. 1993. The evaluation of the capital region policy and a few policy suggestions. *Housing Studies.* 1, 2: 87-112. In Korean.

Yoo, H.W., D.M. Ryum, and W.H. Cheong. 1995. *Land Administration in the Localization Era.* Anyang: KRIHS. In Korean.

Wilson, P. 1997. Building social capital: a learning agenda for the twenty-first century. *Urban Studies.* 34: 745-760.

DONG-HO SHIN

Governing Inter-Regional Conflicts: Managing Expansion in Pusan, Korea

T here is much debate on the role that large cities play in fostering economic growth. For some writers the growth of large mega-urban regions is the prerequisite for economic growth; they provide the institutional and settlement framework in which agglomeration economies reduce transport costs and create greater productivity (See Hamer 1994). On the other hand many commentators regard the growth of these large urban regions as presenting major challenges to sustainable development arguing that the demands that such urban regions place upon the environment, energy supply and material goods threaten global and local viability (See McGee 1999). Whatever the correctness of these arguments there is no doubt that one of the major problems of urban growth which is recognized by all researchers is the problems presented by the rapid expansion of urban activities outwards from the city core (See McGee and Robinson 1995). This spillover into the urban hinterlands causes land-use conflict, environmental problems and the need for expensive transportation and infrastructural investment. Such problems are common in many of the world's leading urban regions but they are especially serious in the rapidly growing cities of Asia, including Korea.(IKLAR 1996; Lee 1992). This expansion also presents major difficulties of urban management as the outwards movement occurs in many different levels of political jurisdiction ranging from rural counties to independent municipalities. This process is also occuring at a time of rapid political change in many Asian countries in which the decentralization of political power to the local level in increasing in conjunction with the greater political empowerment of civil society. This situation creates a critical need for developing new systems of urban management that can resolve the difficult inter-regional conflicts that are emerging in these large urban regions.

Over the past several decades, South Korea has vigorously pursued policies of industrial growth. During this period, traditional urban centers expanded rapidly, and new industrial cities were formed. The administrative area of Seoul, for example, was redefined several times, growing from approximately 270 km^2 in 1960 to 600 km^2 in 1995, while its population increased from 2.5 to more than 10 million over the same period (Kwon 1995). Once a port city of modest size, Pusan is now Korea's second-largest city, with a population of about four million (Shin 1994). As was to be expected, rapid urban expansion has had significant spill-over effects on neighboring regions and has engendered competition and disputes among local governments.

This paper is concerned with the governance of inter-regional conflicts in Korea and the approaches deemed appropriate to tackle them. Using the case of the Extended Metropolitan Pusan Area (EMP), the paper outlines how various levels of goverrnment have attempted to ameliorate the problems brought on by Pusan's expansion (Shin 1995). Of interest here will be the inter-regional Plan for the Extended Metropolitan Pusan Area (PEMP), which covers the city of Pusan and a dozen municipalities in the adjacent province of Kyungnam (Province of Kyungnam et al. 1995).[2] The paper ends with lessons and questions drawn from this experience which may be helpful in dealing with the inter-regional problems of other city-regions in Korea and elsewhere.

Korea's Approaches to Governing
Inter-regional Disputes

As early as 1968, and in response to the need for resolving inter-regional conflicts, the central government created enabling legislation for so-called Associations for Extended Urban Administration (No 1983; So 1998; Son 1983), which provided a loose arrangement whereby two or more local administrative units, acting cooperatively, were enabled to solve inter-regional conflicts. Disputes between and among municipalities, provinces, and metropolitan governments were to be reconciled under the leadership of the national Ministry of Domestic Affairs. Participating parties, however, were not obligated to reach agreement on the issues at hand. Nor were there any instruments to force the concerned parties to comply with such agreements as did emerge.

By 1996, fifty-four associations had been organized, and some of them have continued to be active in reconciling inter-regional disputes (So 1998; IKLAR 1996). Common issues dealt with by the associations included changing traffic routes, deciding on the locations of sewage and waste dumping sites, protecting the water quality of river systems, and altering administrative boundaries. But, by the early 1990s, the more or less relaxed association approach was no longer sufficient. As a result of a broad democratization process in the country, local politics had become more prominent, and intra-regional conflicts flourished. In 1991, the country re-instituted an elected council system at provincial and municipal levels and, after a lapse of thirty years, the first elections for provincial governors and mayors were held in 1995. More forceful, if sensitive, measures were now needed to respond to rising public demands. The formulation of regional plans was one of the alternatives, in addition to the already existing method of conflict-resolution through annexation. Before considering how, and in what circumstances, the new approach was employed, the following section will provide a brief introduction to the geography of the EMP.

Expanding Pusan Metropolitan Region

Pusan and Its Hinterlands

Korea is a small country with a land mass only one-fifth that of California. A coastal city in the southeastern corner of the country, Pusan lies about 500 km to the south of Seoul, and 400 km from Kwangju, another major centre to the southwest (Figure 1). In 1995, Pusan's administrative area was 530 km², having more than doubled in size since 1960 (MoDA 1996). In 1963, Pusan was separated from the province and acquired metropolitan status, equivalent to the authority and rank of a province. Before then, it had functioned as provincial capital and had played a key role as the centre of economic and social activity for the whole of southeastern Korea. The people of Pusan, however, have had to depend upon clean water from Nakdong River, most of whose tributaries flow across the territories of Kyungnam and Kyungbuk provinces north of Pusan. While the total area of Kyungnam is twenty times larger than Pusan, it is similar in the size of its population.

The eastern and southern area of Pusan is enclosed by the sea, but the city's western and northern borders are shared with municipalities in Kyungnam province. Thus, the municipality of Kimhae is located to the west and Yangsan to the north, both being directly affected by spill-overs from Pusan. Major Korean transport systems—trains and highways—terminate at Pusan. Built-up areas of the city are developed along the coastal lines of the southeastern sea, located between the Korean peninsula and the Japanese island of Kyushu.

Once a colonial enclave, Pusan has grown to be a major port city. In addition to its port functions, the city is also one of the major centres of footwear manufacturing in the country. Since the late 1960s, however, the city's economic growth has been stagnant. This was in clear contrast

Figure 1: Geography of Extended Metropolitan Pusan

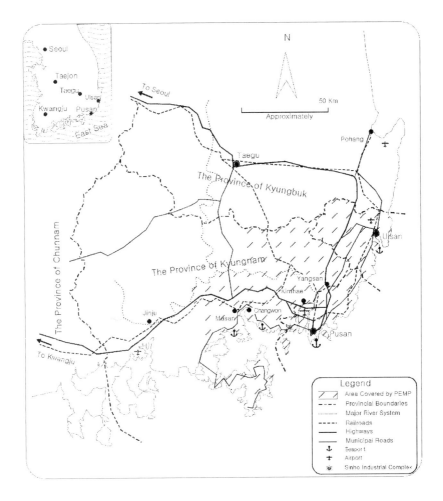

to the rapidly growing industrial cities in and around Kyungnam province, which were strongly assisted by the central government. Secondary centres around Pusan, such as Ulsan, Pohang, and Changwon developed rapidly. Together with areas adjacent to them, they form a vast industrial region which some authors call the "Southern Industrial Belt" (Markusen and Park 1993). Along with its core city of Pusan, the Belt has sometimes been regarded as balancing the national space economy against the behemoth capital of Seoul.

Pusan's Dilemma

The most serious problems for the metropolitan area of Pusan have been its stagnant economy and urban congestion. As already mentioned, Pusan had become heavily dependent upon footwear production and commercial activities by the late 1960s (Lim 1993). By that time, however, the international competitiveness of the city's manufacturing base was already declining. With the Korean government focusing attention on the development of petrochemical and machinery industries, Pusan lost out in government funding. Even worse, the city's economy was negatively affected by the general increase in wages. With economic growth proceeding throughout the 1980s, labor costs had risen significantly, making it difficult for Pusan's light industries to compete.

By 1980, several of the major employers in Pusan went bankrupt, among them corporate giants such as Kukjae, Dongmyung Timber, and Yunhap Steel and Iron. For example, before it went under, the Kukjae group had ranked among the top five Korean conglomerates. Although political factors had influenced the shutdown, the economic circumstances of the city had become critical.

After the major companies closed down, Pusan's economy, especially in manufacturing, continued on a downward slope. The size of enterprises, the amount of value added by the firms, and their production capacity all had poor showings relative to other regions. For example, in 1985, Pusan's Gross Regional Product (GRP) per capita had stood at 93.5 percent of the Korean average (BoS 1993), but a decade later it had declined to 76 percent (BoS 1996). Pusan's poor economic performance contrasted unfavorably with Kyungnam province's accelerated growth, whose per capita GRP in 1995 exceeded the national average by 34 percent.

The second factor that made Pusan's dilemma more serious was the lack of developable land. Both of the city's southern and eastern borders are enclosed by the sea, while its western and northern sides are bounded by mountains. Many of the mountainous areas within its jurisdiction are inappropriate for urban expansion, and the city has been unable to provide inexpensive lands for either urban infrastructure or industrial use.

And finally, as the quality of life within the city began to decline, people as well as firms started to move out of the city into Kyungnam province (Table 1). The situation had become serious. The city was losing both population and economic base.

With the general exodus from Pusan, municipalities such as Yangsan and Kimhae (see Figure 2) were rapidly industrializing. Yangsan, across the city limits of Pusan to the north, grew from a population of 70,000 in 1990 to 163,000 in 1995, while Kimhae to the west expanded from 166,000 to 255,000 over the same period (BoS 1996).

Table 1: Firms and Jobs Moving Out of Pusan to Surrounding Areas

Years	1987-88	1989-90	1991-92	1993-1994
No. of Establishments	37	201	203	213
No. of Employees	1906	6948	15552	6673

Figure 2: Inward and Outward Migration between Pusan and its Hinterlands

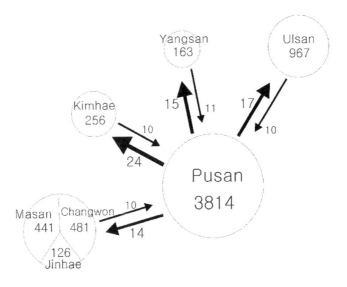

Notes: The number in each circle indicates the population size of the city, and the number along each arrow indicates the number of people who migrated in 1995 (based on BoS 1996). All numbers are in thousands.

The growth of these newly developing hinterlands of Pusan and the major industrial cities beyond them, such as Pohang, Ulsan, and Changwon, began to coalesce, forming a dynamic Extended Metropolitan Pusan (Markusen and Park 1993). Both within this region, and between it and the rest of the country, flows of people and materials increased. For instance, the traffic volume on six major roads to and from Pusan leaped from 59,000 vehicles in 1986 to 275,000 in 1995, a gain of 466 percent (MoCT 1986, 1995) and, on east-west roads across the EMP by a staggering 867 percent. Daily commuters within the EMP also increased. During the decade beginning from 1980, the number of outward-bound commuters from Pusan soared by 260 percent (BoS 1980, 1990), by more than doubling even this phenomenal growth. All of these movements over an outdated transport system contributed to congestion, necessitating heavy outlays on infrastructure. The dramatically growing car ownership in Korea has only made things worse.[3]

Efficient transportation in the EMP is considered to be a national problem, with Pusan handling 40 percent of Korea's exports (CCIP 1997). Although road connections around the region were continuously upgraded, the poor accessibility of Pusan's port system failed to be corrected. Worsening accessibility and the accompanying increases in the costs of transportation eventually led the national government to intervene in the governance of the EMP.

Kyungnam's provincial government concurred that Pusan's problems would have to be solved. As part of a healthy metropolitan economy, the province hoped to be able to form a counter-weight to the heavy concentration of economic power in the capital region of Seoul. However, the concerned parties strongly disagreed among themselves about whose interests should be sacrificed in moving towards solutions. Extending urban transit lines, creating new roads, developing industrial lands as well as housing and resort complexes, and locating waste dumping sites, were all highly contentious proposals. As a result, the entire planning process can be regarded as a battle between metropolitan Pusan and Kyungnam province about who should bear the financial, environmental, and social costs.

The Battle

In South Korea, three major regional groupings divide most organizations engaged in political, social, cultural, and economic activities (Kim, M.J. 1989; Lee 1998). Over a history of more than a thousand years, these divisive regionalisms have been competing among each other, at no time more intensively than during the past three decades. Physically, they are broadly identifiable with the way the country is sectioned off by mountain ranges. (For its part, Seoul is not commonly seen as a separate region in this sense, perhaps because its population is a mixture of the three). Many people consider traditional regionalism in Korean history a major impediment to national progress.

Kyungnam and Pusan, however, have the same regional identity. Despite this, rivalry and even a certain antagonism between them is strong, reflecting primarily differences in local interests. In earlier stages of the city's growth, the Pusan government attempted to solve its perennial problem of land shortage by expanding its territory. Even after its separation from Kyungnam, three successful attempts were made to incorporate a total of approximately 370 km^2,[4] by annexing Kyungnam's lands, needless to say over the strenuous opposition of the province.

The first attempt to enlarge its territory took place in 1978, when some parts of Kimhae were incorporated into the city. A second attempt followed in 1989, when further portions of Kimhae were transferred. Most of these were underdeveloped rural lands. The third attempt to expand Pusan's territory was initiated in 1994 and completed during the period of the PEMP process two years later. Led by national assemblymen representing Pusan, this potential "land grab" became one of most contentious regional disputes. But in spite of strong opposition from Kyungnam, the annexation was again successful. This time, the area transferred was a portion of Yangsan, for a total of about 115 km^2. Although the area was not especially valuable for urban development, the incident contributed to the erosion of the cooperative spirit of Kyungnam officials.

Further efforts to annex Kyungnam lands, this time, however, without changing administrative boundaries, were made through the formal inter-regional planning process of the PEMP. Initiated by Pusan in 1994, the PEMP was strongly supported by the central government. Pusan, in fact, had been preparing to engage in some form of macro-regional planning for some time. The first round was initiated by Pusan's Chamber of Commerce and Industry with two reports, released respectively in 1988 and 1992 (CCIP 1988, 1992). A third report was produced by the Institute of Pusan Development Systems, a private consulting firm owned by a powerful local politician (IPDS 1992). The Institute made specific recommendations for the city's future and was comparable in quality to the CCIP reports. However, none were acted upon at the time, though material from all three studies surfaced again in the PEMP.

The Central Government's Resolutions

Based on the unfavourable evaluation of the association approach (So 1998), and in response to the rapidly increasing inter-regional disputes around large urban centres in the mid-1990s (Cho 1996), the Ministry of Construction and Transportation promulgated the "Law of Balanced Growth and the Promotion of Local Small-and-Medium Scale Enterprises." The "balance" in the title implied a need for the coordination of, and cooperation among, developmental activities between large urban centres and their outlying areas. The new law gave the Ministry a legal basis for initiating inter-regional plans such as the PEMP, and in 1994, the Ministry stepped in to deal with the spill-overs of large cities and the disputes resulting from them, beginning with Pusan.

At the start of the PEMP process, the Ministry of Construction and Transportation contacted both Kyungnam province and the city of Pusan.

It wanted to use the PEMP as a model for applying the new Law of Balanced Growth. Prior to the official process at the governmental level, several reports on the problems of Pusan had already been produced to suggest solutions that would have required cooperation between the two local government entities. One of them was a planning exercise conducted by two neighboring research institutions, the Pusan Development Institute (PDI) and Kyungnam Development Institute (KDI). Representing their respective governments, the two institutes undertook a joint research project on the governance of the EMP.[5]

Although the Construction Ministry was officially in charge of the whole planning process, the Korean Research Institute for Human Settlements (KRIHS), a *de facto* subsidiary of the Construction Ministry, worked on the elaboration of the plan. At the local level, the PDI and KDI were mobilized to gather data and to develop policy alternatives responsible for their respective governments. A contract was signed by the Ministry and the KHRIS to create the PEMP and, as sub-contractors, PDI and KDI took part in the process. Based on previous research on the affected region of Pusan (CCIP 1992, 23-29), the planning boundaries of the plan were drawn to cover the whole area of Pusan along with fourteen adjacent municipalities in Kyungnam, an area that, in 1992, included six and a half million people. This planning region included all of the major cities of Kyungnam province—Ulsan, Changwon, Kimhae and Masan—and approximately 40 percent of its land mass. Most of the areas were located within the distance of 60 km from the core city, Pusan.

Ideas and research results from earlier reports, such as those by the Chamber of Commerce of Pusan (1988, 1992), the Institute of Pusan Development Systems (1992) and the Province of Kyungnam (1992), along with new demands from each government, were used by KRIHS in drawing up the final plan. Obviously, both provincial governments were anxious to place the largest possible number of developmental projects within their own jurisdiction. In the case of Pusan, the government and the PDI tried to persuade KRIHS planners to locate industrial sites, large distribution centres, a "teleport," golf courses, and an additional seaport in Pusan. On the other hand, the city persistently pursued placing projects such as waste dumping and sewage treatment centres *outside* its boundaries. For its part, Kyungnam tried to take advantage of the planning process, proposing large developmental projects, such as an international airport, a greatly improved and expanded port system, a new town, and so on. The province also attempted to develop new housing and industrial sites adjacent to its boundary with Pusan to take advantage of potential spill-overs. On the other hand, it rejected the idea to expand the capacity of water reservoirs on the Nakdong River within its own jurisdiction, which was being proposed to meet Pusan's increasing need for water. These arguments were vehemently pursued not only among different levels of local government, but also among other stakeholders in Kyungnam and Pusan.

Despite these disputes, there were also promising signs. Communications flowed not only vertically between central and local levels as they had in the past, but also horizontally among government units at the same level. Public officials and local council members relied heavily on the planning institutions of their own localities to come up with innovative ideas and solutions, while central planners made efforts to obtain local knowledge by contacting bureaucrats and key persons in various social organizations. Indeed, the process of collaborative planning raised the esteem in which especially local planning institutions were held (see Figure 3). And the media also contributed by raising people's awareness of planning and the choices it involved.

Once the preliminary plan had been drafted, the Construction Ministry called a few meetings to mediate remaining inter-ministerial conflicts at the central level, and inter-governmental conflicts at the local level. In these meetings, the Ministry successfully persuaded the concerned

Figure 3: Institutional Mechanism of Creating the PEMP

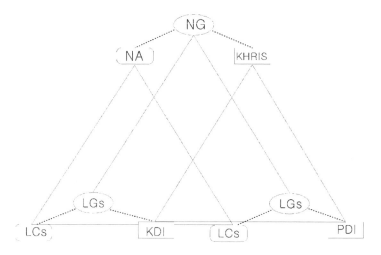

Notes: NG: National Government; LGs: Local Governments; NA: National Assembly; LCs: Local Councils
Source: by author's observation

parties to accept its decisions as binding. The most intractable issues, however, such as the location of landfills and sewage treatment centres in Kyungnam, were not even mentioned. Instead, the Ministry incorporated their locations into the plan only *after* the formal meetings had concluded, and without publicity of any kind. This proved to be an enormous shortcoming.

The PEMP was finalized in late 1994, and the plan was released in April of the following year (MoCT et al. 1995). It included a number of development projects, such as a teleport, new towns and industrial sites, expansions of both the subway system and roads, and upgrading railways, seaports, airports, etc., many of which would be of benefit to both regional governments. Since the publication of the plan, some of these projects have been built, such as the Industrial Complexes of Sinho and Noksan[6] and the New Town of Jangyu in Kyungnam province. The Samsung Automobile Company, a new car manufacturer, has located its factory in the Sinho area, beginning production in March 1998. A container deposit serving the Pusan port was built in Yangsan, and several road systems have been improved and/or newly constructed.

To be sure, some of these projects had been started already prior to the PEMP. On the other hand, the construction of landfills and sewage treatment centers, one of the most urgent needs of the region, has yet to begin. Perhaps the secrecy surrounding their site selection was a factor in this delay. Furthermore, the unexpected economic crisis of 1997 has led to the postponement, if not cancellation of many regional projects. For all these reasons, it is not clear whether the plan has, in fact, made a significant difference for the region. In the end, the implementation of projects seems to depend more upon the will and financial abilities of related national ministries than upon the plan itself.

Conclusions

In this paper, I have described the processes of expanding urban centres and the approaches taken to resolve the increasing problems resulting from an expanding metropolitan region in Korea. It has focused on governing inter-regional disputes related to the EMP, the core of Koreas second largest industrial region. Three approaches were briefly examined: association, annexation, and planning. What can we learn from this experience extending over four decades?

Regarding the resolution of inter-regional disputes, I would conclude as follows. First, the collaborative planning approach that was finally adopted is a more reasonable way of overcoming inter-regional disputes than any of the preceding attempts. Using the PEMP process, the

Ministry of Construction and Transportation successfully managed disputes that had existed since the 1950s and, over the years of economic and political transformation, had grown into exceedingly complex challenges. With the Law of Balanced Growth, it created a legal basis that might be used by any urban government for a similar purpose. Even though the Ministry employed some undemocratic measures, its mediation was largely successful. A complete evaluation of the PEMP will have to be based on several years of plan implementation. Even so, it is already clear that the PEMP has built a robust institutional framework for collaborative planning that is applicable also to other Korean cities. Several of these have already been initiated.[7]

Pusan's historical strategy of simply annexing neighboring territories in a desperate effort to reverse its economic decline will probably not be repeated. The future lies rather with collaborative planning (Healey 1998). This is, of course, only as far as procedure is concerned. Choosing the right industrial policies is just as important and perhaps more so. In the era of information economy, policies will have to focus on high-level services and flexible specialization rather than the manufacturing industries of the rigid command and control era of the past (Castells and Hall 1994; Piore and Sabel 1984).

Notes

[1] The Korean government is a unitary system, in which three levels of government are legally recognized. The highest is the central, or national, while the provinces and the municipalities are operated at the local level. Throughout this paper, the "local government" is used to mean metropolitan, provincial and municipal governments. The metropolitan government has a status equal to the province, and the term "central" and "national" governments are used interchangeably in this paper.

[2] The region covered by this plan includes fourteen municipalities within Kyungnam province and the city of Pusan as a whole. It is a counter magnet of the Capital Region, where more than six million people reside. The details of this will be introduced later.

[3] The number of automobiles registered for Korea increased from 2.7 million to 7.4 million (approximately 280%) only in five years between 1989 and 1994 (based on BoS 1995), for example.

[4] This is compared to 373 km^2 of Pusan's total land mass in 1970, and 749 km^2 in 1997.

[5] The outcomes of these activities were presented at semi-academic seminars held at each of the two regions, one in Pusan and the other in Changwon, the capital of Kyungnam. See KDI (1994), for example.

[6] Industrial complexes of Noksan and Sinho were planned for development of 9.4 and 3.1 km^2 of industrial lands, respectively.

[7] Extensive planning studies have been completed for Taejon-Chungju (MoCT et al. 1996) and for the Kwangyang-Jinju region (Province of Chunnam 1996).

References

Amsden, A.H. 1990. South Korea's record wage rates: labour in late industrialization. *Industrial Relations.* 29: 77-93.

Bureau of Statistics (BoS), Republic of Korea. 1980. *Census of Population and Housing.* In Korean.

Bureau of Statistics (BoS), Republic of Korea. 1990. *Census of Population and Housing.* In Korean.

Bureau of Statistics (BoS) Republic of Korea. 1995, 1996. *Korean Statistical Yearbook.* In Korean.

Bureau of Statistics (BoS) Republic of Korea. 1993, 1996. *Gross Domestic Regional Products.* In Korean.

Castells, M. and P. Hall. 1994. *Technopoles of the World: Making of Twenty-first-century Industrial Complexes.* London: Routledge.

Chamber of Commerce and Industry of Pusan (CCIP). 1988. A *Study on Directions of Development for Pusan Metropolitan Region.* In Korean.

Chamber of Commerce and Industry of Pusan (CCIP). 1992. A *Study on the Characteristics of Pusan Metropolitan Region.* In Korean.

Chamber of Commerce and Industry of Pusan (CCIP). 1993. 1997. *Index of Pusan's Economy.* In Korean.

Chamber of Commerce and Industry of Yeosoo (CCIY). 1986. A *Study on Industrial Relocation of the Extended Kwangyang Bay Region.* In Korean.

Chamber of Commerce and Industry of Yeosoo (CCIY). 1990. *The Future of Development in the Extended Kwangyang Bay Region.* In Korean.

Cho, M.-R. 1996. Regional conflicts in the era of local autonomy. *Community Development Review.* 21, 1: 27-40. In Korean.

Friedmann, J. 1998. Rethinking urban competition and sustainability in East Asia. *Sustainable Urban Competitiveness: Rethinking East Asian Cities,* Proceedings of Seoul Metropolitan Fora 98, held 27-28 May 1998, University of Seoul. 13-28.

Gottmann, J. 1961. *Megalopolis: The Urbanized Northeastern Seaboard of the United States.* Cambridge, MA: MIT Press.

Hamer, A.M. 1994. Economic Impacts of Third World Mega-Cities: Is size the issue? *Mega-City Growth and The Future.* Edited by R.J. Fuchs et al. Tokyo. United Nations University Press, 172-191.

Healey, P. 1998. Collaborative approaches to urban planning and their contribution to institutional capacity-building in urban regions. *International Journal of Urban Science.* 1, 2: 167-183.

Hong, D.-S. 1989. Social backgrouds and regionalism. *Korean Regionalism and Regional Conflicts.* The Society of Korean Sociology, Sungwonsa Publishing Co., 59-73. In Korean.

Hong, K.-H. 1996. *Regionalism and Korean Politics.* Seoul: Backsansudang Publishing Co. In Korean.

Institute of Korean Local Administration Research (IKLAR). 1996. An Evaluation on the Management of Integrated Urban-Rural Cities. Seoul. In Korean.

Institute of Pusan Development Systems (IPDS). 1992. An Exercise of 5-year Planning for the Pusan-Kyungnam Regional Development. Seoul. In Korean.

Kim, M.-J. 1989. The formation and characteristics of Korean regionalism. *Korean Regionalism and Regional Conflicts*. The Society of Korean Sociology, Sung-Won-Sa Publishing Co, 153-165.

Kim, W.-B. 1989. Industrial restructuring and related labour issues in Korea. *IDS Bulletin*. 20, 4: 32-46

Kwon, Y.W., and J.W. Lee. 1995. Spatial patterns of migration in the Seoul metropolitan area. *Journal of the Korean Planners' Association*. 30, 4: 21-39. In Korean.

Kyungnam Development Institute (KDI). 1994. *Development Planning Ideas of Pusan-Kyungnam Extended Metropolitan Area*. KDI Policy Discussion Paper 94-2. In Korean.

Kyungnam Development Institute (KDI). 1996. *Impacts of the Development in Western Pusan on its Hinterlands in Kyungnam and Long-term Perspectives for Kyungnam*. KDI Research Report. In Korean.

Lee, J.-R. 1992. Impacts of the location of industrial complex on regional transformation). *Journal of the Korean Planners' Association*. 27, 3: 117-133. In Korean.

Lee, K.-Y. 1998. *Korean Elections and Regionalism*. Seoul: Oh-reom Publishing Co. In Korean.

Lim, C.-H. 1997. The change in metropolitan settlement patterns and its implications for planning concepts and policies: the case of Seoul metropolitan region. *Journal of the Korean Planners' Association*. 32, 5: 297-316. In Korean.

Lim, J.-D. 1993. Urban growth and industrial restructuring: the case of Pusan. *Environment and Planning* A. 25: 95-109

McGee, T.G. 1999. Urbanization in an Era of Volatile Globalization:Policy Problematiques for the 21st Century. *East West Perspectives on 21st Century Urban Development*. Edited by J. Brotchie et al. Aldershot: Ashgate, 37-52.

McGee, T.G. and I. Robinson. 1995. *The Mega-Urban Regions of Southeast Asia*. Vancouver: University of British Columbia Press.

McGee, T.G. 1991. The emergence of Desakota regions in Asia: extending a hypothesis. *The Extended Metropolis in Asia*. Edited by N. Ginsburg, B. Koppel, and T. McGee. Honolulu: The University of Hawaii Press, 16-17.

Markusen, A., and S-O Park. 1993. The state as industrial locator and district builder: the case of Changwon, South Korea. *Economic Geography*. 69: 157-181.

Ministry of Construction and Transportation (MoCT) Republic of Korea et al. 1995. *The Plan for the Extended Metropolitan Pusan*. In Korean.

Ministry of Construction and Transportation (MoCT) Republic of Korea et al. 1996. *The Plan for the Extended Metropolitan Taejon and Chungju*. In Korean.

Ministry of Construction and Transportation (MoCT) Republic of Korea. 1986, 1990, 1995. *Statistical Yearbook of Road Transportation*. In Korean.

Ministry of Domestic Affairs (MoDA) Republic of Korea. Various Years. *Yearbook of Korean Cities*. In Korean.

Moon, S.-N. 1989. Historical backgrounds of regional disparities in Korea. *Korean Regionalism and Regional Conflicts*. The Society of Korean Sociology Sungwonsa Publishing Co., 33-44.

No, Y.-H. 1983. Administration of extended metropolitan regions: the current situations and policies for resolving problems. *Municipal Affairs* 18, 7: 8-18. In Korean.

Park, S.-O., 1993. Industrial restructuring and the spatial division of labor: the case of the Seoul metropolitan region, the Republic of Korea. *Environment and Planning* A. 25: 81-93.

Park, S.-Y. 1990. *Principles of Urban Administration*. Seoul: Pakyoungsa Publishing Co. In Korean.

Piore, M. and C. Sabel. 1984. *The Second Industrial Divide*. New York: Basic Books.

Province of Chunnam. 1996. *Comprehensive Development Plan for the Kwangyang Bay Region: A Final Report*. Kwangju, Korea. In Korean.

Province of Kyungnam. 1992. *The Second Comprehensive Development Plan for the Province of Kyungnam*: 1992-2001. Changwon, Korea. In Korean.

Pusan Development Institute (PDI). 1994. *Alternatives for Using Areas for Receiving Migrating Firms from Pusan and Mobilizing Financial Resources*. In Korean.

Shin, D.-H. 1994. *The Impacts of Industrialization on the Quality of Life in Korea: Case Studies of Ulsan and Kyungju*. PhD dissertation, University of British Columbia, Canada.

Shin, D.-H. 1995. The processes and contents of planning for the extended metropolitan Pusan region. *Journal of the Korean Planners' Association*. 29, 4: 44-45. In Korean.

So, J.-K. 1998. Current situations and tasks for implementing extended metropolitan administration in Korea. *Issues and Perspectives on Promoting the Economy of the Mid-Land Area*. Proceedings of Conference of the Korean Regional Development Association, 20-21 February 1998, Hannam University, Taejon, Korea. In Korean.

Son, J.-M. 1983. Current situations and alternatives of inter-urban administrative association. *Municipal Affairs* 18, 7: 19-32. In Korean.

TOSHIO KAMO

Urban-Regional Governance in the Age of Globalization: The Case of Metropolitan Osaka

T he closing years of the twentieth century are witness to an unexpected economic turmoil in most of East Asia which, until recently, had been regarded as the preeminent growth region of the world economy. Some of the advantages which East Asia had enjoyed, such as lower investment costs, uncontrolled capital markets, high levels of export, and so on, suddenly diminished or actually turned into disadvantages. This dramatic turn-around in market conditions was the fundamental reason why the "East Asian Miracle" (World Bank 1993) was suddenly transformed into the "East Asian Crisis."

Urban-regional governance systems in East Asia had for decades been obliged to adapt to processes of mega-city formation. Starting from centralist-interventionist systems that had put national governments either directly in charge or control of urban administrations, governance systems for the metropolis were frequently reorganized, evolving new institutions (Ruland 1996). Reorganizations throughout this period were generally undertaken to manage hyper-rapid growth. But under today's conditions of economic decay, new ideas and governance systems are needed to mitigate economic distress.

To some extent, Japanese cities in the 1990s have been undergoing similar changes. In retrospect, even in the 1970s, when "urban decline" was becoming a major concern in advanced countries, Japan was said to be a notable exception. Except for a small number of old industrial cities, Japanese cities were continuing to grow right up to the beginning of the present decade, with Tokyo in the lead. Although Osaka, Japan's second most important city, found itself in a somewhat disadvantaged position vis-à-vis the capital region, its economy continued to expand along with the rest, carried forward by the overall dynamic of the national economy.

Growth in both cities, however, slowed down and eventually stopped altogether once the notorious "bubble economy" had burst. Manufacturing, formerly construed as the engine of economic and urban growth, was beginning to decline in both Tokyo and Osaka prefectures (TMG 1995; OPIAID 1997), as car and electronic assembly operations moved overseas. In addition, financial institutions, particularly those of foreign origin, relocated from Tokyo to places such as Singapore and Hong Kong, which they found to be less costly and less regulated business environments. In the phrase of the day, Japan's metropolitan economies were "hollowing out" (TMG 1996).

As a result of these far-reaching changes, urban-regional policies in Japan had to shift from a growth-promoting pattern to one of distress-management and structural reform. Deregulation of foreign investments to revitalize financial markets, retrenchment of the public sector to respond to the fiscal crisis and diminish the tax burden on the private sector, and achieving a new industrial mix to reflect changes in the international division of labor were the principal policy measures adopted in the new "age of distress."

This article examines the characteristics of this turn-around in urban-regional governance in Japan through a case study of metropolitan Osaka.

The Urban Regional Governance System in Postwar Japan

The central-local relationship in the postwar period could be characterized as a "centralized authority-dispersed function" system (Kamo 1997). Although local governments were operating on a large scale, their administrative and fiscal autonomy was actually quite limited. During the growth-stage of the economy, this system had worked effectively in that it concentrated resources at the centre and were then reallocated across the country. The current system of urban-regional governance was gradually evolved within this context. A knowledgable foreign observer, Norman J. Glickman, described this system in straightforward terms. In Japan, he wrote, "regional planning [is] organized along the [top-down] principle, with national goals and organizations dominating those on regional and local levels" (Glickman 1979).

To be sure, planning for land use, development, infrastructure, and environmental management was organized hierarchically from the national level on down. Central government agencies, such as the National Land Agency (NLA) and Economic Planning Agency (EPA) periodically drafted and redrafted both the National Comprehensive Development Plan (NCDP) and the national economic plan in consultation with various central ministries as needed. NCDPs, in turn, were broken down to plans for specific regions such as the Capital and Kinki-Kansai regions. In preparing these plans, sub-units of the central government would consult with major local governments in their respective areas, but the legal right to decide on the plans remained with the centre. Based on these plans, local governments elaborated their own comprehensive plans, with separate chapters on land use, economic development, social welfare, environment, public health, education, etc. These plans were meant to be subordinate to the central government's national and regional planning directives, and the administrative and fiscal regulatory mentioned above worked to secure this top-down relationship.

Plan implementation worked roughly as follows. Sub-units of central government agencies along with quasi-public corporations were in charge of all national projects at the regional level, such as the construction of highways, ports and airports, energy facilities, and public housing. Local governments, either individually or in collaboration, undertook to carry out projects indicated in their own plans but always in conformity with the state's comprehensive regional plan. Finally, at each regional and local level, federations of economic associations, chambers of commerce, and occasionally labor unions and certain private sector groups joined with local governments in promoting their plans. This complex, hierarchically structured, and interdependent public-private system formed the regional governance system in postwar Japan (Kamo 1990).

The Political Economy of the "No. 2 Region"

The growth-oriented urban-regional governance system in Osaka-Kansai

The designation "Kansai" requires a brief explanation. Historically, "Kinki" and "Kansai" were used interchangeably, although "Kansai" had a somewhat vaguer connotation. Today, however, "Kansai" is the official name of a legal-administrative region composed of eight prefectures: Osaka, Kyoto, Hyogo, Nara, Shiga, Wakayama, Mie, and Fukui. In this region, the three dominant cities, Osaka, Kyoto, and Kobe, each have more than one million population, with Osaka leading.

Throughout the postwar era, the economic status of Osaka Prefecture as the second-richest city in the national urban hierarchy, has declined relative to national totals (Table 1).

For this reason, the prefecture and other local governments along with business communities in the Kinki-Kansai area tried repeatedly to "catch up" with Tokyo and revive the bi-polar (Tokyo-Osaka) geographical pattern that had prevailed until the early part of the century. In a sense, it was nostalgia for the olden days when Osaka-Kansai was one of the top two city-regions of the nation that drove local government and business leaders to be the equal of Tokyo once again. Tokyo became the model to emulate. In the 1950s, for instance, Osaka's government, working hand in

Table 1: Concentration of Socio-Economic Activities
(shares of Tokyo in the nation %)

	Year	Tokyo Region	Tokyo Prefecture	Tokyo Wards Area
Number of Corporate Headquarters	1980	59.4	53.3	
	1993	58.3	51.2	
Persons Engaged in Publishing/Advertising	1981	48.3	41.4	50.1
	1993	50.1	39.3	36.6
Bank Loan Outstanding	1980	45.8	43.5	
	1994	52.3	43.5	
Persons Engaged in Foreign Banks	1981	85.6	84.7	
	1991	91.7	91.6	91.6
Persons Engaged in Foreign Firms	1981	77.4	65.8	
	1991	76.8	66.7	63.9
Persons Engaged in Academic and R&D	1981	45.3	21.3	13.0
	1991	41.6	18.0	11.4
Number of Theaters	1981	22.1	13.9	
	1991	28.5	17.8	
Persons Engaged in Cultural Occupations	1975	53.3	37.7	
	1985	50.2	31.3	

Source: National Land Agency

hand with the local business community, promoted a project for building a huge heavy-industrial base in the Sakai and Senboku industrial zone on Osaka Bay. This was followed in the 60s by a plan to invite the World Exposition to Osaka, an attempt to "catch up" with Tokyo which had hosted the 1964 Olympics and, in preparation, had succeeded in modernizing its infrastructure. The Exposition was held at Osaka in 1970. Some ten years later, an enlarged coalition of local governments and business associations was organized to build two "flagship" projects: the Kansai International Airport and Kansai Science City. At the time, Tokyo's role as a "world city" was becoming evident, facilitated by the construction of Narita International airport and Tsukuba Science City. In imitation of Tokyo, the projects that the Osaka-Kansai region undertook during the 1980s were intended to intensify the global functioning of the region as a whole.

The institutional structure of urban-regional governance in the Osaka-Kansai area, however, was different from Tokyo's in two major respects. Whereas Tokyo's government was metropolitan in scope, combining central city wards and prefecture, in Osaka, city and prefecture were governed separately. The second difference was in the degree of central government involvement. In Tokyo's case, the central government always played an important and often decisive role in the development of the Capital Region. Narita International Airport, for example, was constructed entirely with state funds and was subsequently managed by a state-owned corporation,while the Tsukuba Science City was developed mainly by moving national university and research institutes from Tokyo's central city towards to a peripheral location. The Association for Consolidation of the Capital Region (ASCR) was also a state-initiated organization.

By contrast in Kansai, public-private partnerships dominated, involving, on the side of the public sector, both national and local governments. The new airport was turned over to be managed by a joint-stock corporation. Similarly, Kansai Science City was developed primarily through a partnership arrangement. Without a strong presence of the state, regional governance in Kansai was less effective than Tokyo's. For example, the Council for Promoting the Development of Kinki (CPDK) consisted of eight, later enlarged to nine, prefectures and three large cities in and around the Kinki-Kansai area. Established in 1960 under the catch phrase of "Kinki is one," it was actually a fragmented and internally competitive organization reflecting the fact that "Kinki was not one, but many." In sum, the urban-regional development system did not work as well as it might have done. The centralist-statist philosophy of "the nation's capital is special" clearly put Osaka at a disadvantage. On the other hand, it is also true that the region had a more collegiate form of governance that avoided the excesses of the top-down Tokyo model.

An Intermission of Growth-Oriented Governance

The Osaka-Kansai's urban-regional governance system described above was devised as a vehicle for a pro-growth politics. Priority was given to economic development, and financial resources were allocated chiefly to land development, the construction of industrial sites, the port, and other economic infrastructure. With much less flat area available for industrial expansion in Osaka than in Tokyo, drastic land development projects such as leveling whole mountain sides and reclaiming parts of the Osaka Bay were carried out with serious environmental impacts.

As in other East Asian countries through the 80s and early 90s, the building of mega-cities had been one of the driving forces of Japan's economic growth from the beginning. The emergence of these gigantic cities entailed social and environmental degradations, however, that gave rise to a number of social movements opposed to single-minded economic growth. In the early years, chaotic mega-city formation had spawned social and political unrest and eventually, in both Kansai and Tokyo, left-wing political parties, supported by labor unions, environmentalists, and incipient civic movements took over local governments in the region. In Kansai, the prefectural governments of Osaka and Kyoto, together with the cities of Kobe, Kyoto, and a number of others came to be ruled by anti-growth coalitions. Accordingly, the 1970s came to be called an era of "progressive" local government. Government priorities shifted from the single-minded pursuit of economic growth to social welfare, education, environmental protection, and democratization (Steiner, Kraus and Flanagan 1980). But despite its real achievements, the "progressive" block of Osaka, along with that of Tokyo, was still politically too immature to successfully govern on a regional scale. When a fiscal crisis struck in the mid-70s, and with internal fissions within the progressive block itself, the left was defeated in the 1979 local elections. Not surprisingly, the growth coalition was back in the saddle.

New Evolution of Urban-Regional Governance of Osaka-Kansai

As pointed out, despite the presence of CPDK and other intergovernmental arrangements and public-private partnerships in Kansai, actual relations among local governments were not especially harmonious until well into the 1970s. For example, both Kyoto and Kobe were proud of their identities as cities and reluctant to join Osaka-led development projects. Relations between Osaka Prefecture and Osaka City were also characterized by rivalry. And yet, to promote huge projects such as the international airport and the science city, an efficient division of labor among participating governments, along with a willingness to work together over the long haul, were essential. In addition, the central government had to become more committed to the region, and larger contributions from the private sector were also required.

Responding to this situation, KEF and Osaka Prefecture, backed by the NLA—a central government planning agency—initiated a move to build a new Kinki-Kansai-wide planning scheme in the early 80s. By 1987, this initiative had materialized as the "Subaru (Pleiades) Plan: Toward the Creation of a New Kinki," which turned out to be a long-term regional development plan. The area it covered was identical with the jurisdiction of the CPDK, and the actual planning body was called the "Creating New

Kinki Committee" (CNKC). The Committee was composed of the nine prefectures and three large cities of the region, with participation of representatives from the business and academic communities (CNKC 1987). Thus, a new framework for the urban-regional governance system of the Osaka-Kansai area was being formed.

The Coming Age of "Glocalization"

From "Kansai Renaissance" to "Kansai Crisis"

The 1980s was the period when Tokyo's emergence as a world city first became evident. The Fourth National Comprehensive Development Plan, announced in 1987 under the Nakasone administration, proposed certain policies to promote the "world-cityness" of Tokyo and in the expectation that his would turn Japan into a powerful centre of the global economy. But the Osaka-Kansai "establishment" complained that too much attention was being paid to the capital region and demanded measures that would facilitate Kansai's aspiration to share world-city status with Tokyo. Among the projects being proposed were the international airport, the science city, an Osaka stock market, the International Garden and Greenery Exposition of 1990, and the APEC Osaka Meeting to be convened in 1995. All were part of the "World-City Kansai" initiative.

Indeed, in the late 1980s, the projected investments for Kansai surpassed those in the Tokyo area. At the time, then, the new system of regional governance based on the "Subaru Plan" appeared to be working quite effectively in terms of its own understanding of "success." For the first time since the end of the war, the region's share of leading national economic and financial indicators had increased slightly (Table 1). And when catch phrases, such as "Kansai Renaissance," "Kansai Is Back," and "The Challenge of Osaka," started to appear in newspaper and magazine headlines, many people believed that the Tokyo-centered polarization of Japan's economy was drawing to an end.

When the Japanese economic "bubble" burst in the early 90s, however, the losses sustained in Kansai were as serious as those in Tokyo. In fact, on some criteria—the decline in land values, number of bankruptcies of financial institutions, the fiscal crisis of local governments—was among the most serious in the nation. Above all, by the mid-90s, the deficit in the Osaka Prefecture budget was the worst among all of the country's 47 prefectures. Needless to say, urban-regional policies would have to change.

How did this dramatic turn-around in performance and expectations come about? Quite simply, because development projects during the preceding decade had speculated on the future and lost. In general terms, the present malaise of Japan's economy can be explained by aspects that are peculiar to Japan's political economy, such as excessive state regulation, market closure, an incompletely articulated financial system, and so on. But leaving these questions aside, the most acute factor unquestionably is an *excess of investments* in so-called development projects. For a number of decades, the percentage of public sector capital formation in GDP had been four times that of the United States. Public investment was being employed as an easy way to generate domestic demand and accelerate the upward movement of the business cycle. As a result, land values rose sharply, and speculative investments in real estate expanded. These can be said to be the principal causes of Japan's high-cost economy and put industrial investments in harm's way. Kansai was one of the most extreme cases of this speculative syndrome. The region's development boom of the 1980s was the prelude to hardship in the following decade.

New Reforms in Regional Governance

New moves for reforming Kansai's regional governance system appeared in due course. In 1998, KEF, together with four economic associations (Osaka Chamber of Commerce, Kansai Economic Fraternity Association, Osaka Manufacturers Association, and Kansai Corporate Managers Council) proposed to consolidate the CPDK, Subaru Plan Committee, and other regional associations into an integrated, region-wide, public/private consortium to be called the "Kansai Council" (KC). The major difference from previous arrangements was that the KC was to have a comprehensive research, planning, project-promoting, coordinating, and consensus-building function. The policy areas to be covered are equally ambitious: culture, tourism, public relations, disaster prevention, environment, industrial development, and the promotion of science and technology.

The background to this move was threefold: the decentralizing reform of the governmental system overall, further advances of globalization, and the fiscal crisis of local government. In regard to the first, the reform of the postwar system of "centralized authority-dispersed function" system had become urgent. Overconcentration in Tokyo, and the inefficiencies of the highly complex, hierarchical system of central-local relations had become untenable. Everyone, from the business community to local governments, political parties, and the mass media supported a move to decentralization. After the regime change of Japanese politics in 1993, which ended the LDP's monopoly as the governing party, the national Diet enacted the Decentralization Promoting Act (DPA). Soon afterwards, the Committee for Promotion of Decentralization (CPD), which had been established by the DPA, made a series of recommendations for reform. And although the central bureaucracy resisted furiously and, to some extent, succeeded in holding on to power, central-local relations are gradually being transformed into a less hierarchical system.

This change entails more intense inter-city and inter-regional competition than before. It is notable that, in this instance, KEF assumed the role of an initiator of decentralization. In doing so, it proposed to create a new, more effective local-regional governance system for enhancing Kansai's power. Indeed, KED hoped to abolish the prefecture system, replacing it with a region-wide governmental body and, at the same time, consolidate some smaller municipalities into larger units. Because of the practical difficulties of implementing such a drastic reform, KEF is, for the present at least, taking a more flexible approach. Creating the Kansai Council was proposed in this context: KEF apparently believes that the Council can become a stepping stone for creating a regional government.

Continuing globalization in the 1990s was also a force driving governance reform in Kansai. Despite the "World-City Kansai" campaign mentioned earlier, the economic difficulties of the decade meant that the world-city notion might not actually produce the benefits expected. Tokyo is still the principal gateway connecting Japan with the global system. And other cities are also running hard. Nagoya, for instance, has strengthened its position in the domestic urban hierarchy because of Toyota's presence and the investments occasioned by the World Expo Nagoya. And, because of its links with South Korea and Taiwan, the Fukuoka-Kyushu area is also in a relatively favored position. Amidst this intensified interregional rivalry, Kansai needed new instruments for further globalizing its economic base. One of these was a more effective and efficient regional governance system (KEF et al. 1998).

Finally, the fiscal situation of local governments in Kansai is at present so serious, that they are quite unable to respond to the needs of the global age. Osaka Prefecture is suffering the most severe problems. With massive debts incurred by excessive public investments in the 80s and early 90s, the prefecture is close to losing its ability to run the metropolitan area on a day-by-day basis. For the first time in its history, it is currently undergoing stringent fiscal retrenchment. To make matters worse, adjacent Hyogo Prefecture and Kobe City, both major players in Kansai, have not yet fully recovered from the damage of the Hanshin earthquake of 1995. Cities within Osaka Prefecture are also in bad shape. In terms of a balanced budget criterion, four or five of them have for a number of years appeared on the nation's "worst ten" list.

The public sector in the Osaka-Kansai area is thus simply in no condition to undertake new initiatives. Still worse, its ability to manage the social distress arising from the economic crisis is limited as well. Prefecture budgets for social welfare and public health have had to be reined in. Many prefectural responsibilities have been transferred to the municipalities under the guise of "decentralization," at the same time that the municipalities themselves are reluctant (if not actually unable) to assume them. Nor can prefectures expect help from a national government that is itself suffering serious fiscal problems at the same time that it is supposed to revive the national economy and is being pressured to come to the aid of struggling East Asian countries.

"Big Is Efficient" vs. "Small Is Beautiful"

Current changes in the Japanese governmental system are quite contradictory. Both central and local governments are required to balance their budgets at a time when fiscal resources are needed to underwrite the aging of the Japanese population; yet they are also being pressured to mobilize new resources to stabilize financial markets and to start up the real economy as well. As for local governments, they are being pressured, on one hand, to assume new responsibilities which would make them more independent and accountable and, on the other, to respond to global forces by inventing strategies for regional cooperation.

Partly in answer to these contradictions, KEF and allied business groups are proposing a reform that would create a regional governing body with comprehensive powers. With the support of the governing party (LDP), a similar coalition at the national level is also moving in this direction. Ideas such as reducing local-level administrations to one-tenth their present number, and replacing the 47 existing prefectures with about a dozen regional (provincial) governments are becoming influential. In terms of local government, Japan is currently in the thrall of a "big is efficient" philosophy.

But is "big" really efficient? And can enlarged local-regional government provide a solution to the problems outlined above? Research by an Osaka institute with which I am involved found that the assumption is unwarranted. It is true that, correlating *per capita* working expenditures of local government with size of population, *per capita* expenditures diminish as the population of local jurisdictions increases. Fiscal efficiency would thus be improved by enlarging jurisdictions. But *this is true only up to a certain point*, past which the efficiency curve flattens out and eventually starts to decline. Based on data for local governments in Osaka Prefecture, the turning point appears to lie between 100 and 200 thousand people (Kishiwada Urban Policy Institute 1998). If we now assume, as some have proposed, that local governments are reduced to one-tenth their present number, the average size of a locality in Osaka

Prefecture would be about 400 thousand. According to our findings, massive local government consolidation would therefore not improve fiscal-administrative efficiency but actually make it worse! If this result is confirmed, the "big is efficient" idea may well turn out to be a myth.

As I argued in the introductory section, Japan is now struggling to get through the present crisis and is seeking to adjust the country's political economy to a global standard. Restructuring via decentralization, retrenchment, outsourcing, and consolidation is being introduced at all governmental levels. And Osaka-Kansai is no exception. But what if the "big is efficient" logic should turn out to be wrong? Osaka Prefecture's population is as large as Sweden's, and Hyogo's population size (inclusive of Kobe City) is equal to that of an average American state, while the average size of local authorities in Japan is 38,000. The case for keeping things relatively small is thus a strong one. Economies of scale may well turn into diseconomies. Moreover, in a post-Fordist era, flexible networking is needed not only in factories but also in government, particularly in agencies concerned with social welfare, public health, and the environment. If this line of argument is accepted, Kansai's business community and incumbent prefectural administration would be better advised to consider a flexible form of planning and policy coordination in place of creating a new form of mega-government. The 1995 earthquake taught an important lesson in this regard.

When the disaster happened, the traditional "centralized authority-dispersed function" system initially failed to respond. Because of complex interdependent central-local relations, neither central nor local authorities could set rescue operations in motion, as each side waited for an initiative of the other. In the absence of a meaningful governmental response, the earliest rescue operations were undertaken by community-based organizations.

Subsequently, in caring for victims and slowly returning to a resumption of normal life, smaller governmental units were more effective than larger ones. For example, evacuation camps were closed first in the small towns of Awaji Island, followed by middle-sized cities in the Hanshin area, and last in the area's largest city, Kobe. In small towns, people knew each other closely and could help in more meaningful ways , whereas ward officials in larger cities had no personal knowledge of whom they were supposed to help, and so adopted bureaucratic procedures that were less effecatious. From this experience, one could conclude that smaller governmental units and community-based people's organizations work better when a crisis strikes.

The same thing could be true in the case of day-to-day services for the elderly and handicapped. The coordination of inter-governmental programs is certainly needed, but so is a flexible, intimate service delivery in today's governance systems. In this sense, "small is more beautiful" today than ever before.

In response to such a need, municipal governments in Kansai, along with those in other areas, are gradually moving to a more decentralized system of planning and decision making, particularly in social and environmental areas. Welfare, public health, and community development plans (and programs) are being devolved to neighborhood levels, encouraging citizen participation. Neighborhood councils and other community-board institutions, already existing in western Europe and North America, are beginning to spring up also in Japan. But even as this is happening, the "big is efficient" idea in the economic sphere, with its implicit centralization of governmental functions, continues to prevail.

This contradiction has not yet been resolved. The huge voluntary action which emerged in the wake of the earthquake demonstrated the great strength of civil society in Japan. Inspired by that, arguments for legislation to facilitate NPO and NGO activities surged throughout the nation. Subsequently, a so-called NPO-bill was introduced in the Diet and, after three years of discussion, was finally enacted in 1998. The new NPO Act is very conservative, however, in that the qualifications of an NPO are narrowly restricted and no tax abatement is granted. This shows that the postwar bureaucratic system in Japan continues undaunted, limiting reforms percolating from the bottom up.

Needless to say, the "big is efficient" and "small is beautiful" principles are not absolutely incompatible. The coming age of "glocalization"— the merging and interpenetration of the global with the local—requires institutions that would make them compatible. But, for the time being, Osaka-Kansai's regional governance system is moving chiefly along the well-defined path of the past.

Conclusion

Despite the rather pessimistic tone of this paper, it is worth mentioning that Kansai is a still a big economy, with a regional GDP as large as Canada's. Although a certain amount of "hollowing out" has occurred, the region still harbors a large number of small to medium-sized firms that are using advanced technologies and are closely linked with the Asia-Pacific region (Hill and Fujita 1998). Local governments and the business community in Kansai have strategies to enhance these linkages, as exemplified by Osaka City's Business Partnership Program and the Osaka Prefecture's Asian-Pacific Business Center Plan, both being policy measures to assist the region's smaller firms to find business opportunities through intercity networking. In a sense, Osaka-Kansai is more open to foreign direct investments and imports than any other region in the country, precisely because of its position as No. 2 in the national urban hierarchy. If this relative disadvantage can be turned into an advantage, Osaka-Kansai might yet have a future as the nation's most open, globalized region. In order for this to happen, however, the region needs a more balanced form of governance, combining economic with social effectiveness.

References

Cohen, M.A. 1996. The Hypothesis of Urban Convergence: Are Cities in the North and South Becoming More Alike in an Age of Globalization? *Preparing for the Urban Future: Global Pressures and Local Forces.* Edited by M.A. Cohen, et al. Washington, DC: Woodrow Wilson Center.

Creating New Kinki Committee (CNKC). 1987. *Subaru Plan: Toward the Creation of New Kinki.* Tokyo. In Japanese.

Glickman, N.J. 1979. *The Growth and Management of the Japanese Urban System.* New York and London: Academic Press.

Hill, R.C. and K.F. 1998. Osaka's Asia Linkages Strategy: Regional Integration in East Asia, Local Development in Japan. *Urban Affairs. Review.* 33, 4.

Japan External Trade Organization. 1997. *The Asian Currency Crisis.* Tokyo. In Japanese.

Kamo, T. 1990. Metropolitan Government System in Transition: Tokyo and Osaka. *Great Cities of the World,* Vol.7 : Tokyo and Osaka. Tokyo: Institute of Economic Research, Osaka City University. In Japanese.

Kamo, T. 1997. Time for Reform? Fifty Years of the Postwar Japanese Local Self-Government System. *Japan: Eyes on the Country.* Foreign Press Center.

Kishiwada Urban Policy Institute. 1998. *Urban Policy Kishiwada,* No. 4. In Japanese.

Kansai Economic Federation et al. 1998. *The First Report on the Great Sphere Coordination in Kansai.* In Japanese.

Osaka City. 1996. *Outlook of Osaka City.* In Japanese.

Osaka City. 1997. *The Guideline for Promoting Internationalization of Osaka City.* In Japanese.

Osaka Prefecture. 1995. *The Strategy for Promoting Industries of Osaka.* In Japanese.

Osaka Prefecture. 1997. *Overview of Osaka Prefecture, Japan*

Osaka Prefectural Institute for Advanced Industrial Development (OPIAID). 1997. *White Paper on the Osaka Economy.* In Japanese.

Ruland, J., ed. 1996. *The Dynamics of Metropolitan Management in Southeast Asia.* Singapore: Institute of Southeast Asian Studies.

Steiner, K., E.S. Kraus and S.C. Flanagan, eds. 1980. *Political Opposition and Local Politics in Japan.* Princeton: Princeton University Press.

Tokyo Metropolitan Government (TMG). 1995. *Labor and Economic Statistics.*

Tokyo Metropolitan Government. 1996. *Report on the Effect of Industrial Hollowing-Out.* In Japanese.

The World Bank. 1993. *The East Asian Miracle.* Washington, DC: World Bank.

Transborder Regional Governance and Planning: The Case of Singapore and its Neighbors

As far as we know, there is no literature on how local governments design institutions regarding cross-border matters (Veen and Boot 1995, 80).

The Rise of Cross-border Flows in Asia

The timing, intensity, and variety of cross-border flows, and the implications of these flows for the economic integration of regions in the Asia Pacific have been a major focus for urban and regional studies in the 1990s. Aside from the example of Singapore and its neighbors, which is my case study for this paper, much has been written about the Hong Kong and Taiwan's connection with southern China (Henderson 1991; Maruya 1992; Klintworth 1994). Other initiatives are being reported in northeast Asia, the Yellow Sea Rimlands involving the two Koreas, China and Japan, and the Tumen Economic Development project involving Russia's Far East, China, Japan and Korea (Kim 1990, 1991; Manguno 1993; Chen 1995).

The increase in cross-border flows is the outcome of both political and economic forces. Borders which were once meant to contain inter-country tensions now become entry points, as the Asia Pacific region becomes more secure, ideological differences yield to more pragmatic considerations (Scalapino 1992), and new institutional arrangements mediate differences, promoting cooperation between neighbors (Regnier et al. 1991). The economic dynamic that drives cross-border flows includes, most significantly, the growth of intra-Asian foreign direct investment as Taiwan, Korea, Singapore increasingly invest their economic surpluses in the places they know best, that is, their immediate neighboring regions (Ho and So 1997).

The issue I deal with in this paper is not with the timing or the causes of cross-border flows, but with their management, both in terms of facilitating them and as efforts at regulation to contain possibly negative consequences arising from cross-border movements of people, goods and investments. In particular, Veen and Boot (1990) observe that there has been little research documenting how governments design institutions that oversee cross-border matters. Following Kantor et al. (1996), I examine the conditions that empower governments, but focusing on cross-border regimes. My interest is not only in their formation but also, in the specific case of Southeast Asia, in the conditions that inhibit their further development. By taking a comparative perspective, I show how Asia lags behind other parts of the world in efforts at building multinational governance institutions capable of managing cross-border flows. The reasons for the underdevelopment of regional regimes of governance are examined, and the strategic economic and political considerations for different levels of governments are discussed.

SIJORI Cross-border Cooperation in a Comparative Perspective

From the case of Singapore-Indonesia co-operation in the SIJORI Triangle, it can be seen that joint developments have been carefully restricted to self-contained projects, whether in the form of an industrial park, a golf course or recreational resort. There has been very little movement towards the creation of genuine transboundary institutions or towards the harmonising of national laws in the sub-region. (Grundy-Warr and Perry 1996, 198-199)

Singapore's involvement in developing the border regions of its two closest neighbors, Indonesia and Malaysia, is arguably the most developed form of cross-border cooperation in East and Southeast Asia. The term "SIJORI" is a combination of the prefixes of the regions involved in the cooperation, namely **SI**ngapore (a city-state), **JO**hor (the southern most state in peninsular Malaysia) and the **RI**au islands, particularly Batam, Bintan and Karimum (the cluster of Indonesian islands nearest to Singapore). Several issues are relevant in a comparison of the SIJORI project with other cross-border efforts.

Political motives and economic cooperation
The concern for the under-development of border regions has been the historical impetus of inter-state regional cooperative ventures (Hansen 1986). And, within a national context, border regions, often a major focus of national security concerns, and are frequently marginalized economically, precisely because they occupy a geographically peripheral position (Veen and Boot 1995). The desire to stabilize peripheral regions via

economic development thus forms one of the main thrusts of regional development. The U.S.-Mexico maquiladora (twin plant or production sharing) programme is an example of this, with its aim of developing the more economically depressed regions on the Mexican side of the border (Fatemi 1990). Similarly, German policy has targeted underdeveloped border regions for special assistance (Anderson 1990).

SIJORI, by contrast, involves a city-state and regions in two neighboring countries at different levels of development, an economic integration process that is similar to Hong Kong and southern China (Ho and So 1997). However, with Hong Kong's political integration with the People's Republic of China, inter-regional relations have entered an interesting transitional phase. While issues of national interest will now be decided by Beijing, the fact that Hong Kong has been declared a special administrative region means that a border of a certain kind still exists. On either side of it, economic, political differences will persist, reflecting different institutional arrangements. Cross-border flows will be an outcome of these differences. For example, Hong Kong companies will continue to take advantage of spatial disparities by moving labor- and land-intensive manufacturing operations to southern China, while retaining for itself critical sales and administrative functions in close proximity to producer services (advertising, financial, legal, etc.).

The SIJORI initiative, on the other hand, involves three state systems, at both local and national levels, governing sub-regions with very different economic profiles. Already one of the more densely populated and economically richer states prior to the formation of SIJORI (Kamil et al. 1991), Johor looks at cross-border cooperation as a strategy to restructure its economy, turning from primary production to manufacturing and higher value-added activities.

In contrast to Johor, the islands of Riau[1] had, until recently, largely a rural orientation. Prior to 1970, the islands were engaged in fishing and subsistence agriculture, with some primary processing (e.g. sawmills) and mining, while a small ethnic Chinese community maintained trade relations with Singapore (mainly in Tanjung Pinang, Bintan island). Although the Indonesian government has made several efforts to develop the islands economically (especially in Batam), dramatic changes occurred only during the past decade. An economic survey published in the mid-seventies mentioned the intention of the central Indonesian government to turn the islands into an export processing zone, but added that the zone "is unlikely to have much of an impact on the rest of the Province, at least for some time to come" (Esmara 1975). In 1973, Batam had a population of only 6,000. But with many infrastructure projects completed recently, the growth indicator summarised in Table 1 are indeed impressive.

Thus, rather than a border characterized by common underdevelopment on both sides, it is the unequal development existing at three adjacent locations that drives cross-border cooperation, with Singapore needing to expand its economic space, and Johor and Riau able to contribute land and labor of various categories.

Table 1: Growth indicators for Batam, Indonesia

Indicator	1985	1995
Local Workforce	6,159	117,156
Ship Calls	5,592	63,009
Aircraft movements	1,545	13,766
Tourist Arrivals	60,161	936,402
Export Value (us$mill)	11.4[1]	353.9

Source: Batam Industrial Development Authority 1997
Note: [1] (1996)

Recent history of cooperation

The maquiladora (twin plant or production sharing) industry in the U.S.-Mexican border represents a 35-year history of border cooperation and longer, if we consider that the maquiladora program replaced the earlier "bracero" program (Warner 1990). Transborder cooperation in the North American Alantic Northeast represents one of the most advanced forms of regional para-diplomacy, with Canadian premiers and American governors meeting regularly on cross-border issues, with follow-up by policy staff (Duchacek 1990). Likewise, the national borders of Europe provide many examples of inter-state transborder cooperation. For example, the Regio Basiliensis region straddling France, Germany and Switzerland had a history of cooperative efforts beginning in 1963 (Briner 1986). Other European examples include the border cooperation between France and Italy (Minghi 1991) as between Sweden and Finland (Vartiainen and Kokkonen 1995).

In contrast, the SIJORI project was only initiated in 1989 and formalized in 1994. It should be noted that diplomatic relations among Singapore, Malaysia and Indonesia have a very short history of less than 50 years, since all three countries are until recently, British and Dutch colonies. The relations between these three countries continue to be haunted by a memory of the past. "Singapore is a dagger pointed at our breast.

Singapore must be crushed" was a sentiment attributed to a high ranking Indonesia (Hanna 1960) reflecting the strain in Indonesia-Singapore relations after the Indonesian independence in 1949. Tensions culminated in a military confrontation by Indonesia against Malaysia and Singapore in 1963. Singapore's separation from Malaysia two years later was also the result of a long period of conflict, from differences in political styles, economic interests and ethnic composition. It was only in 1967, with the formation of ASEAN as regional body, that relations between the three countries moved back to a more tentative, cordial state.

Thus, the recent cross-border cooperation has to be understood within a larger context of newly independent states, and more importantly, of states which have almost as long a history of conflict as collaboration with each other. The chilling relations between Malaysia and Singapore in 1996 over the Singapore Senior Minister remark about crime in Johor, despite an immediate apology, and the 1998 dispute over the relocation of the Malaysian railway customs office in Singapore, as well as the use of Singapore's port for Malaysian cargo illustrate how far the two neighbors have still to go in dealing with the management of conflict between them.

National versus local government initiatives[2]

There is by now a growing literature on the rising activism of local states in looking overseas to attract foreign investment as a response to increased global competition. Part of this drive is a result of of local states' disenchantment with the ineffectiveness of the federal form of government—both Indonesia and Malaysia having that structure (Soldatos 1990). Expanding state capabilities, and the increased realisation that exports, direct foreign investment, and tourism are crucial to its economic viability, have added to local activism (Fry 1990). As a result, scholars point to the rise of city-states and the need, more generally, for cities to shift their focus from traditional housekeeping to an entrepreneurial role. As Eisenger (1989, 9) argues, there is a need for the local state to "identify, evaluate, anticipate and even help develop and create markets for private producers to exploit, aided if necessary by government as subsidizer or co-investor." Looking inward, Pierce et al. (1993) argue the need for city and suburban authorities in the United States to work together, along with other interests, in developing effective governance at the regional level. Looking even further inward and drawing on his experience as former mayor and state legislator, Rusk (1995) calls for a revival of American cities by calling on state governments to unify local authorities, and create what he calls regional metro-governments.

Part of this new activism is the attempt by sub-national governments to increase cross-border economic exchanges to mutual benefit. The U.S.-

Mexican border cooperation on economic and environmental issues involves, on the U.S. side, 25 counties in the states of California, Arizona, New Mexico, and Texas, and, on the Mexican side, 35 municipalities in the states of Tamaulipas, Nuevo Leon, Coahuila, Chihuahua, Sonora, and Baja California (Arreola and Curtis 1993; Ganster 1998). Similarly, in the European case, it is sub-national governments that are most active in cross-border cooperative efforts.

SIJORI, by contrast, represents an initiative among three national governments. In Indonesia's case, central government involvement has meant the possibility of changing the regulatory environment facilitate new development in peripheral regions. This is most clearly seen with the amendments in property ownership laws and changes in land leases. There were also early hopes of standardizing immigration controls and remove import duties in order to facilitate a freer flow of people, goods, services, and information across the Triangle (*Straits Times*, 31 May 1991). However, the free flow of commodities and factors of production within the Triangle remains an idea that has so far not been explored by the various governments.

The involvement of national governments from Indonesia and Malaysia in the SIJORI project requires a way of inserting their respective provincial governments into the project. Coordination problems have cropped up. On the Indonesian side, because Pekanbaru (the capital of Riau Province) is located on the mainland in Sumatra, there is the danger of a split in SIJORI ventures between mainland and island interests. As mentioned earlier, SIJORI projects are focused on the islands closest to Singapore rather than on the whole of Riau Province. The interests of the Riau governor, on the other hand, are primarily tied to his larger and more immediate constituency on the mainland. This orientation is clear from Governor Soeripto's comment that "as economic co-operation and development in the Riau Islands is running smoothly, now is the time for us to extend it to the mainland" (*Straits Times*, 19 November 1991). This comment by the governor, together with an earlier one relating to the urgent need to develop the agricultural sector, points up one danger: the possible displacement of regional realities by national priorities so long as national governments are in the lead. Aside from this divergence of interest, the distance of Pekanbaru prevents the provincial government from dealing effectively with the impacts on Riau island communities. An added complication has been the different Indonesian state agencies involved in the development of different islands and their competing development visions, for example, regarding the place of labor-intensive projects in Riau's development (*Straits Times*, 20 April 1993, 23 April 1993, 3 May 1993).

The multiple involvements of the central government and the awkwardness in which the Indonesian sub-national government has reacted to the SIJORI initiative reinforces Grundy-Warr and Perry's (1996) observation that appropriate transboundary institutions are badly needed in Southeast Asia. In the second half of this paper, I examine this problem in greater detail, first by looking at the actual collaborations that have occurred. Have these been, as Grundy-Warr and Perry have argued, essentially a series of self-contained projects, or are there more promising efforts at transboundary institutionalisation? Secondly, I look at the issue of the regional governance process in the wider context of interests among the actors involved in cross-border cooperative ventures, both in terms of the cross-cutting interests of the three countries, and also from the viewpoint of central versus sub-government interests.

Transborder Regional Governance and Planning

A transborder regime is a set of rules and institutions, formal and informal, which aim at and succeed in regularising neighborhood behaviour. (Duchacek 1986, 18)

If we expand on Duchacek's definition of a transborder regime, then it is important to realize that rules and institutions provide for the articulation of cross-border agreements between neighboring countries. While rules specify what is possible and what actions may be taken, we need to look further to the level of agencies and cross-border organizations to see how broad agreements and intentions to cooperate are operationalised into practical realities. We have several examples from various border regions. AykaV (1994) for example, points out that, in Europe during the 1950s and 1960s, technical transfrontier commissions with well defined powers and specific mandates had begun to emerge, while the 1970s and 80s saw the growth of cross-border planning committees. In the case of Regio Basiliensis, a German-French-Swiss government commission formed in 1975 to oversee regional cooperation, delegated specific matters to two regional committees and their respective working groups (Briner 1986). Another European example, the AlpAzur, exists to help local governments to represent border issues to the central governments of France and Italy (Minghi 1994). In the first half of the 1980s, the governors of the four American and six Mexican border states organised as the Border Governors Conference meeting annually, established six standing committees to operate in the intervening periods (Gress 1996). The U.S.-Mexican Border Environmental Co-operation

Commission represents a more specific agency tasked with the function of facilitating environmental infrastructure projects such as waste water management in the border region (Varady et al. 1996).

Has the SIJORI region developed to this level of inter-governmental cooperation with cross-border associations, inter-state commissions, and similar institutional arrangements to handle cross-border issues? In answering to this question, a number of points may be noted:

1. Since the SIJORI agreement was reached nine years ago, all projects have been bilateral in nature, involving Singapore and one of its partners, Riau or Johor. A remaining problem has been the lack of direct involvement between Riau and Johor (Abdullah 1996).
2. The SIJORI initiative has allowed the participating governments to cooperate on joint venture projects in Johor (light industry) and Riau (light and heavy industry). By creating an industrial landscape, these projects will pave the way for Singapore-based and other firms to relocate some of their operations to these areas. Because the Riau islands are largely greenfield sites, cooperation has also involved the provision of infrastructure, notably industrial parks, housing and recreational amenities, and even ferry services from Singapore.
3. While the agreements are made between the participating governments, the operational side is left to private organizations in the form of joint ventures. The longest and most successful partnership is the Batamindo Industrial Park (BIP), a joint venture between Indonesia's Salim group, and two Singaporean companies, Singapore Technologies and Jurong Town Corporation International.
4. The principal focus of the Batimindo Industrial Park is obviously on attracting long-term tenants to the Park. The nature of the Singapore-Indonesian collaboration is clear from the case of Batamindo. The Indonesian part of the collaboration concentrates on the acquisition of land for the 320 hectares for the Park, the sourcing of workers on behalf of its clients and, at the level of working with local authorities, to obtain the necessary permits and licenses. The former general manager of the Park pointed out that a company that signs with BIP can expect to be operational in the Park within three months (interview 9 April 1998). This fast start-up period is an important attraction for potential clients.
5. As an industrial park, Batamindo's purpose is similar to other industrial parks. The only difference is that it involves another country in managing the organization. From the Singaporean viewpoint, BIP represents an export of Singapore's planning standards and project management. In this respect, diplomacy at the level of bilateral

government agreements is essential during the planning phase of the project, by ensuring that the host country is agreeable to Singapore planning standards. Specifically, JTC International, one of the joint venture partners tasked with building the Park, essentially relied on their extensive planning experience in building industrial estates in Singapore. This is most noticeable in its factory designs (four standard types, with a fifth, custom built, option) which were gleaned from JTC's experience in building factories in Singapore, as well as town planning in terms of the provision and siting of a wide variety of amenities, creating an integrated and comprehensive estate including not only factories and associated infrastructure (power plant, sewerage, water treatment, etc.), but also facilities for its inhabitants (worker quarters, food, health, entertainment, etc.).

6. Diplomacy is also necessary because of the concept of self-sufficiency. In order to maintain the production standards and schedule of multinational companies, the Park created a total environment in which all inputs necessary for production (water, power, telecommunications, workers, housing, etc.) are provided. Their constant supply by BIP allowed industrial operations to run without the possibility of external interruptions, another attraction for potential investors.

7. It is this mixture of central government involvement at the level of diplomacy and government-linked organizations at the level of operations that facilitated the development of the Riaislands. BIP represents the link between diplomacy and actual operations and, in turn, is connected to a wider network of agencies that, in effect, constitute the cross-border economic governance structure. Thus, in the development and marketing of the island, BIP works closely with the Batam Industrial Development Authority (BIDA). Subsidiaries of BIP also play an important role in developing warehousing and transport services.

8. However, as one element in the cross-border regional governance structure, BIP has an economic mandate to establish a viable infrastructure conducive to production; this mandate, however, does not include social and environmental concerns. For example, a recent report (Peachy, Perry and Grundy-Warr 1997) discusses the problem of illegal housing caused by migrants from other parts of Indonesia who arrive in Batam in search for work, the untreated waste from illegal settlements contaminating water supplies, the erosion caused by massive land clearance schemes, and the growing prostitution problem fed by a large male migrant population as well as clients from Singapore. BIDA, tasked with the infrastructure development of the island, had done an impressive job in the development of roads,

reservoirs, and the telecommunications system. But, again, as in the case of BIP, social and environmental problems do not fall within the scope of its responsibilities. And the Batam mayor's office, which traditionally is expected to deal with these matters, has been strained beyond capacity by the pace of island transformation.

9. This illustrates an ongoing problem with the SIJORI initiative. Economic interests continue to dominate. A set of agencies is in place, charged with economic development, and there has been effective cross-border collaboration between the relevant authorities. On the other hand, social and environmental problems are left to local authorities to deal with. By contrast, environmental problems that become a major transborder issue, as was the haze caused by the recent forest fires in Indonesia, are presented as an ASEAN problem and deliberated by the Environment Ministers of ASEAN countries. Yet again, in a third variation, the thousands of Indonesian illegal workers moving into Singapore and Malaysia in search of work are treated as a simple bilateral issue between the central governments affected. Presently, there are no cross-border agencies to deal with the immediate problems of the SIJORI borderlands.

10. While SIJORI, as the name implies, is a tri-partite arrangement, we note that the evolving governance structures involve only two parties. Abdullah (1996) points out that the Singapore-Riau Ministerial committee would need the inclusion of Johor. Moreover, the bilateral Singapore-Johor Business Council, which has been inactive, shous of Indonesia who arrive in Batam in search for work, the untreated waste from illegal settlements contaminating water supplies, the erosion caused by massive land clearance schemes, and the growing prostitution problem fed by a large male migrant population as well as clients from Singapore. BIDA, tasked with the infrastructure development of the island, had done an impressive job in the development of roads, reservoirs, and the telecommunications system. But, again, as in the case of BIP, social and ecratic societies, the borderline between legitimate transgovernmental behaviour and treason may be unclear (Keohane and Nye 1974, 49)

The absence of a more broad-based, tripartite regional governance structure has to be accounted for in terms of sovereignty issues. At one level, as I have pointed out, this has to do with the actual state of development of inter-state ties, ties that have been haunted by a conflict-ridden past. However, in an attempt to explain the lack of a more comprehensive governance structure, we also need to take into account the relationship between central and subnational governments by asking to what extent authority has been devolved to the subnational level. Again, Europe provides examples. The Swiss constitution, for example specifically authorizes the cantons to engage in transborder activities on matters within cantonal jurisdiction (Duchacek 1990). French and Italian laws allow sub-national governments to engage in various types of collaboration with their counterparts in neighboring countries, provided these do not interfere with central government policies (Weyland 1997). Similarly, German laws now gives the Länder full freedom for microregional transborder cooperation (Gress 1996).

An examination of the Indonesian and Malaysian State systems provide two reasons for the constraints faced by sub-national governments in these two countries. In Indonesia, the central government has almost complete control determining regional development. Tirtosudarmo (1989) suggests that although there are regional development planning boards called B*appeda*, the power of these agencies are superseded by federal sectoral agencies which control the regional development budgets. The implication is that although the regional government may support federal developmental program because of the anticipated economic benefits, the provincial governor functions as "only an extension of the hand of the central government, [their] function more to implement central government demands then to accommodate the needs of the people in the region" (Tirtosudarmo 1989). Thus in the case of Riau, not only is the regional government subservient to the centre, but the direct involvement of the central government in managing the development of the Riau islands (through BIDA in the case of Batam) means that there is little space for the provincial government to come into the operation.

Comparing the national-state government relations in Malaysia reveals some similar features with the Indonesian case, as for example, in the tendency for both central governments to assume the regional planning function, with states essentially acting as its agent and, at best, in an advisory capacity.[3] The particular situation of the Johor state government, however, indicates a number of differences. The Johor government has been quite active in managing industrial development and has been given the power by the Federal government to do so. Historically, through the sale of its water to Singapore, and from the sales of industrial land to Singaporean entrepreneurs, Johor's financial capacity has been healthy, thus strengthening its capacity for intervention in infrastructure and social development. The distance problem (between the border region and the capital) and the mainland-island problem (as with Riau) is also missing in the Johor case. This absence implies that state/national interests are likely to be less divergent than in Indonesia. Moreover, the Johor government has actively intervened by providing housing, roads and amenities such as water and electricity to support the industrialisation effort (Guinness 1990). The activism of Johor State in the early years of the SIJORI initiative has, however, led its Mentri Besar (chief minister of the state) to criticise the central government for its lack of interest in the project (*Straits Times*, 21 September 1992). Although the central government did officially recognise Johor's participation in SIJORI, the minister for trade and industry was reported as saying that the Malaysian side of the three-country cooperative agreement should not be limited to Johor alone (*Straits Times*, 23 May 1993).

A number of reasons have been advanced to explain why the Malaysian central government was initially reluctant to embrace the initiative (e.g., Grundy-Warr and Perry 1996; Jordan and Kanna 1995). But in the light of international experience with cross-border relations, one is led to conclude that in southeast Asia, central governments worry about diplomatic initiatives slipping away from their control to sub-national units which may then develop more intimate relationships with neighboring countries. A remark made by the Johor Mentri Besar in 1990 reflects this tendency: "Whatever the foreign policies of the two countries (Malaysia, Singapore), Johor being the closest to Singapore, would be at the centre. As a result, Johor has to be more realistic in dealing with Singapore. I believe after long years of co-existence, we tend to understand each other better than the people in Selangor" (*Straits Times*, 15 July 1990).[4]

Prospects of Transnational Governance and Planning

> If the nation is to remain globally competitive as it moves towards the twenty-first century, much of the impetus must come from the grass roots… the international activities of state and local governments should expand noticeably in the future as the U.S. economy becomes progressively intertwined with the global economy, resulting in the well-being of local constituencies being linked not only to domestic prosperity but also to the vitality of the international economy. (Fry 1990, 126-127)

As a transborder initiative, and in contrast to the European examples, SIJORI was executed by central governments; sub-national governments had only a minor role. However, Duchacek (1990) argued that flexible multi-centric systems are predisposed to handle problems of global and regional interdependence more effectively than unitary systems.

With very young political systems and an ongoing nation-building effort, all three countries continue to guard their sovereignty closely.

Indonesia, Malaysia, and Singapore have what Duchacek (1990) terms "tightly centralist state systems" where the center exercises a strong rein over its sub-national units as they attempt to secure cooperation across borders. The reaction by both Indonesia and Malaysia has been to appoint ministers from the central government as overseers of the SIJORI initiative. And whereas, in the case of Singapore and the Riau islands, we observed the emergence of a fledging economic transborder governance structure comprised of a network of Singaporean and Indonesian agencies, the sidelining of sub-national governments in the project has meant that a broad-ranging, tripartite governance structure with resources of its own and with regulative powers has yet to emerge.

Within the tight centralist environment in Asia, Singapore has found a particular form of adaptation, working with central governments to obtain concessions in order to develop self-contained, discrete projects. In this division of labor, Singapore exports its technical planning and project management expertise, with national partners handling the regulatory environment, land allocation and labor sourcing process, leaving local authorities to manage social and environmental issues. This model was initially developed with the BIP project, and has now been exported abroad with varying degrees of success.

As indicated in Table 2, Batamindo Industrial Park, the first of these ventures, became operational in 1990. Soon after, two government-linked companies, Singapore Technologies (ST) and Jurong Town Corporation International (JTC Int'l), along with their local partner, the Salim Group, set up the much larger 4,000 hectare Bintan Industrial Estate, with the first phase of 100 hectares operational in 1996. Another company, heavily involved in the development of the Riau islands, is Sembawang, which worked with the Salim Group to develop the Karimun marine and industrial complex of shipyards, steel fabrication and oil terminals. All three companies have continued their collaboration, moving on to more distant shores such as India (Bangalore Information Technology Park), Vietnam (Vietnam-Singapore Industrial Park [VSIP]), and China (Wuxi-Singapore Industrial Park [WSIP], Suzhou Industrial Park), by developing ventures with various local partners. Developing and managing industrial parks in other countries is not without its attendant problems, of course, given the wide variations in the political cultures and regulations of different host environments. However, the logic of starting-up production in a low-wage country and in a highly efficient environment that guarantees a quick start-up and minimal disruptions will continue to appeal.

The sub-national or local government perspective on regional governance is quite different. To a large extent a prisoner of place by

Table 2: Exporting Singapore Planning and Project Management

Park	Year	Size	Singapore	Local Partner
Riau Islands, Indonesia				
BatamIndo	1989	320 hectares	ST, JTC Int'l	Salim Group
Bintan	1st phase 1996	4000 hectares	ST, JTC Int'l Karimun	Salim Group
	1st phase	495 hectares	Sembawang	Salim Group
	1997		JTC Int'l	
India				
Bangalore IT Park	1st phase 1997	27 hectares	ST, Sembawang	Tata Industries
Vietnam				
VSIP HCM City	1st phase 1996	500 hectares (500 reserve)	Sembawang, JTC Int'l	Becamex
China				
WSIP (Wuxi-Suzhou Industrial Park)	1st phase 1995 3 phases to finish in 15-20 years	1000 hectares Municipal Gov't 7000 hectares	ST, JTC Int'l 24 member consortium including ST, JTC Int'l, Sembawang	Wuxi Consortium of 11 Chinese partners

virtue of its limited resources, and subordinated by law to the central government, local states must take Fry's (1990) prescription seriously to develop overseas ties in order to maintain their competitiveness. Thus, the sub-national governments of Johor and Riau must work with their central governments to obtain an arrangement whereby they can become more active in regional and international affairs. At present, with the region in financial crisis, the Johor and Riau governments can perhaps draw an important lesson from the North American maquiladora programme. When Mexico experienced the debt crisis in 1982, followed by the earthquake in 1985 and the 1986 oil price crash, foreign exchange earnings from maquiladoras continued to be healthy, providing the Mexican government with much needed foreign exchange (Zaman 1990). From the Johor and Riau perspective, the SIJORI region may similarly develop into a strong economic region capable of withstanding national economic crises, keeping the participating provinces insulated from the volatility of national economies, provided there are strong cross-border institutions managing the sub-region.

Without some devolution of power from the central government, provincial governments are inherently limited in their ability to chart provincial destinies. Following Fry's (1990) argument, this devolution of power and the empowerment of provinces is necessary to increase the competitiveness of nations, essentially by replacing a central mechanism with a variety of sub-national units, each with the capacity and the potential of creating new opportunities. This process is particularly crucial with border provinces that may require the creation of cross-border alliances for the development of a common sub-region. The empowerment of provincial governments involve the authority to work with their provincial counterparts in neighboring countries to develop transboundary institutions capable of attracting new investments, while having the planning and administrative capacity to monitor and regulate environmental and social problems stemming from rapid economic development.

Notes

[1] It is essential at this point to distinguish between the Riau islands and the rest of Riau province that forms part of mainland Sumatra. It is the Riau islands that are in the original SIJORI agreement. While the rest of the province was subsequently included, it is the islands that experience the rapid industrialization and tourism as a result of inter-state cooperation.

[2] One could make another distinction, and this is on the basis of government versus private initiatives. The Hong Kong and Taiwan efforts into South China are largely individual efforts by small capitalists who rely on kinship and community ties to secure concessions from provincial governments (Smart and Smart 1991; Tung 1994). The differences between diplomacy and *quanxi* are noted in an earlier paper (Ho and So 1997).

[3] See Alden and Awang (1985) for a description of regional planning in Malaysia.

[4] A similar remark was made by a senior official in a top Guangzhou company: "You cannot say that Guangdong is not part of China. But we are closer to Hong Kong and Taiwan than we are to Beijing" (interviewed by *Newsweek* 1992, 12).

References

Abdullah, F. 1996. IMS-GT: Johor's experience. *Growth Triangles in Southeast Asia*. Edited by Imran Lim. Kuala Lumpur, Malaysia: ISIS. 191-204.

Alden, J.D., and A.H. Awang. 1985. Regional development planning in Malaysia. *Regional Studies*. 19: 495-508.

Anderson, J.J. 1990. Skeptical reflections on a Europe of regions: Britain, Germany, and the ERDF. *Journal of Public Policy*. 10: 417-447.

Arreola, D.D., and J.R. Curtis. 1993. *The Mexican Border Cities*. Tucson: University of Arizona Press.

AykaV, A. 1994. Transborder regionalisation: an analysis of transborder cooperation structures in Western Europe within the context of European integration and decentralisation towards regional and local governments. *Libertas paper*. 13. Sindefingen, Germany: LIBERTAS-Europasisches Institut.

Briner, H.J. 1986. Regional planning and transfrontier co-operation: The Regio Basiliensis. *Across Boundaries*. Edited by O. Martinez. El Paso: Texas Western Press, 45-53.

Chen, X. 1995. The evolution of free economic zones and the recent development of cross national growth zones. *International Journal of Urban and Regional Research*. 19: 593-621.

Duchacek, I.D. 1986. International competence of subnational governments: borderlands and beyond. *Across Boundaries*. Edited by O. Martinez. El Paso: Texas Western Press, 11-28.

Duchacek, I.D. 1990. Perforated sovereignties: toward a typology of new actors in international relations. *Federalism and International Relations: The Role of Subnational Units*. (H.J. Michelmann, P. Soldatos, eds.). Oxford: Clarendon Press, 1-33.

Eisenger, P.K. 1988. *The Rise of the Entrepreneurial State*. Wisconsin: University of Wisconsin Press.

Esmara, H. 1975. An economic survey of Riau. *Bulletin of Indonesian Economic Studies*. 11: 25-49.

Fatemi, K. 1990. Introduction. *The Maquiladora Industry: Economic Solution or Problem?* Edited by K. Fatemi, ed. New York: Praeger, 3-18.

Fry, E.H. 1990. State and local government in the international arena. *Annals, AAPSS*. 509: 118-127

Ganster, P. 1998. The U.S.-Mexican border region. 8 pages, *http://wiche.edu/elnet/borderpact/paper/ganster.htm/*

Gress, F. 1996. Interstate co-operation and territorial representation in intermestic politics. *Publius*. 26: 53-71.

Grundy-Warr C., and M. Perry. 1996. Growth triangles, international economic integration and the Singapore-Indonesian border zone. *Global Geopolitical Change and the Asia-Pacific*. Edited by D. Rumley, T. Chiba, A. Takagi, and Y. Fukushima. Aldershot: Avebury. 185-211.

Guinness, P. 1990. *On the Margins of Capitalism*. Oxford: Oxford University Press.

Hanna, W.A. 1960. Pan Malayan relations part I: Singapore and Indonesia— suspicious neigbours. *American Universities Field Staff Reports Service: Southeast Asia Series.* 8: 1-16.

Hansen, N. 1986. Border region development and co-operation: Western Europe and the US-Mexico borderlands in comparative perspective" in *Across Boundaries*. Edited by O. Martinez. El Paso: Texas Western Press, 31-44.

Henderson, J. 1991. Urbanization in the Hong Kong-South China Region: an introduction to dynamics and dilemmas. *International Journal of Urban and Regional Research.* 15: 169-179.

Ho, K.C., and A. So. 1997. Semi-periphery and borderland integration: Singapore and Hong Kong Experiences. *Political Geography.* 16: 241-259.

Jordan, A.A., and J. Khanna. 1995. Economic interdependence and challenges to the nation-state: the emergence of natural economic territories in the Asia Pacific. *Journal of International Affairs.* 48: 433-462.

Kamil, Y., M. Pangestu, and C. Federicks. 1991. A Malaysian perspective. *Growth Triangle: The Johor-Singapore-Riau Experience.* Edited by T.Y. Lee. Singapore: Institute of Southeast Asian Studies and Institute of Policy Studies, 37-74.

Kantor, P., H.V. Savitch, and S.V. Haddock. 1997. The political economy of urban regimes. *Urban Affairs Review.* 32: 348-377.

Keohane, R.O., and J.S. Nye. 1974. Transgovernmental relations and international organizations. *World Politics.* 27: 39-62.

Kim, W.B. 1990. The future of coastal development in the Yellow Sea Rimlands. *Journal of Northeast Asian Studies.* 9: 53-70.

Kim, W.B. 1991. Yellow Sea economic zone: vision or reality? *Journal of Northeast Asian Studies.* 10: 35-55.

Klintworth, G., ed. 1994. *Taiwan in the Asia-Pacific in the 1990s.* Australia: Allen and Unwin.

Manguno, J.R. 1993. A new regional trade bloc in Northeast Asia. *The China Business Review.* 20: 6-11.

Maruya, T. 1992. Economic relations between Hong Kong and Guangdong Province. *Guangdong.* Edited by M. Toyojiro. Hong Kong: Centre of Asian Studies, University of Hong Kong, 26-147.

Minghi, J.V. 1991.From conflict to harmony in border landscapes. *The Geography of Border Landscapes.* Edited by D. Rumley and J.V. Mingley. London: Routledge, 15-30.

Minghi, J.V. 1994. European Borderlands: International harmony, landscape change and new conflict. *World Boundaries.* Volume 3. Edited by C. Grundy-Warr. London: Routledge, 89-98.

Newsweek, 17 February 1992. China's Gold Coast: Is Guangdong too rich for Beijing?" p. 12.

Peachy, K., M. Perry, C. Grundy-Warr. 1997. The Riau Islands and Economic co-operation in the Singapore-Indonesian Border Zone. *Boundary and Territory Briefing* 2, 3. International Boundaries Research Unit, U.K.

Regnier, R., Y. Niu, and R. Zhang. 1993. Toward a regional 'block' in East Asia: implications for Europe. *Issues and Studies*. 29: 15-34.

Rusk, D. 1995. *Cities without Suburbs* Washington: Woodrow Wilson.

Peirce, N.R., C.W. Johnson, and J.S. Hall. 1993. *Citistates: How Urban America can Prosper in a Competitive World*. Washington: Seven Locks, Washington.

Scalapino, R.A. 1992. Northeast Asia—prospects for co-operation. *The Pacific Review*. 5: 101-111.

Soldatos, P. 1990. An explanatory framework for the study of federated states as foreign-policy actors. *Federalism and International Relations: The Role of Subnational Units*. Edited by H.J. Michelmann and P. Soldatos. Oxford: Clarendon Press, 34-53.

Smart, J. and A. Smart. 1991. Personal relations and divergent economies: a case study of Hong Kong investment in South China. *International Journal of Urban and Regional Research*. 15: 216-233.

Straits Times. 1990. S'pore-Johor relations have never been better: Muhyiddin. 15 July, p. 1.

Straits Times. 1991. Johor, Riau and Singapore should harmonise customs rates: Dr Habibie. 31 May, p. 48.

Straits Times. 1991. Riau governor invites Singapore investors to develop province. 19 November, p. 20.

Straits Times. 1992. Federal govt 'sends wrong signals on Growth Triangle. 21 September, p. 16.

Straits Times. 1993. Batam, Bintan slated for high-tech, high-value-added firms. 20 April, p. 13.

Straits Times. 1993. Investors take and wait and see stance on 'new Bintan focus'. 23 April, p. 48.

Straits Times. 1993. No Change to economic plans for Bintan: Jakarta. 3 May, p. 1.

Straits Times. 1993. KL officially endorses Johor's participation in Growth Triangle. 23 May, p. 17.

Sutopo, A.R. 1991. Relations Among Indonesia, Malaysia and Singapore: from confrontation to collaboration and re-alliance. *The Indonesian Quarterly*. 19, 4: 326-343.

Tirtosudarmo, Riwanto. 1989. Central-regional aspects of Trans-migration policy: The Case of Riau. *Prisma: The Indonesian Indicator*. 48: 50-65.

Tung, R. 1994. Taiwan and Southern China's Fujian and Guangdong Provinces. *Taiwan in the Asia-Pacific in the* 1990s. Edited by G. Klintworth. Australia: Allen and Unwin. 154-168.

Vartiainen, P. and M. Kokkonen. 1995. Europe of regions—A Nordic view. *Competitive European Peripheries*. Edited by H. Eskelinen and F. Snickars. Berlin: Springer. 97-114.

Veen, A. van der and D.J. Boot. 1995. Cross-border co-operation and European regional policy. *Competitive European Peripheries*. Edited by H. Eskelinen and F. Snickars. Berlin: Springer, 75-94.

Varady, R.G., D. Colnic, R. Merideth, and T. Sprouse. 1996. The U. S.-Mexico Border Environment Co-operation Commission: collected perspectives on the first two years. *Journal of Borderland Studies*. 11, 2: 89-119.

Warner, J.A. 1990. The sociological impact of the Macquiladoras. *The Maquiladora Industry: Economic Solution or Problem?* Edited by K. Fatemi. New York: Praeger, 183-198.

Weyland, S. 1997. Inter-regional associations and the European integration process. *The Regional Dimension of the European Union*. Edited by C. Jeffery. London: Frank Cass, 166-182.

Zaman, M.R. 1990. The impact of Macquiladoras on Mexico's balance of payments. *The Maquiladora Industry: Economic Solution or Problem?* Edited by K. Fatemi. New York: Praeger, 199-206.

LUCIE CHENG AND CHU-JOE HSIA

Exploring Territorial Governance and Transterritorial Society: Alternative Visions of 21ˢᵗ Century Taiwan

D iscourses on globalization have opened up many frontiers of debates, challenging well-received concepts in the social sciences. Among these are ideas of the state, civil society, identity, nationality, and territoriality, all are elements within what John Friedmann has called territorial governance (Friedmann 1997). The purpose of this paper is to examine the implications of recent theoretical debates on these issues for current visions of Taiwan's governance in the 21ˢᵗ century.

Although the concept of governance, as distinct from government, has been around for sometime, its recent popularity can be attributed to at least four interrelated factors. First is the rising democratic movements in post-colonial countries that gave voice to people's demand for responsive governments through citizen participation. Even in Western democratic countries such as the United States, disadvantaged groups continue to struggle for inclusion and the expansion of democratic rights. Second, associated with this development is the community empowerment or conscientization project which first originated in the Black ghettos of metropolitan cities of the United States, but quickly gained momentum worldwide through the work of Paulo Freire and others (Rozario 1997). Third, environmental, physical and social problems resulting from the continuing and rapid concentration of population in urban areas have overtaken the coping capacity of governments, necessitating their loss of autonomy (Sivaramakrishnan 1996). Lastly, increasing connections of people and non-governmental organizations across territorial boundaries due to globalization has facilitated the growth of, or strengthened local civil societies vis-à-vis their governments. The influence of the concept of governance is indicated by the World Bank's 1994 report entitled *Governance—The World Bank's Experience*. That report lists a transparent process, a professional bureaucracy, an accountable government, a strong civil society, and the rule of law as elements of good governance (World Bank 1994).

John Friedmann, in his call for research on territorial governance of urban regions in the Asia-Pacific (1997), contrasted an "old politics" characteristic of the developmental states of Japan, South Korea, and Taiwan among others, with the "new politics" toward which these states may be evolving. The former was "centralized, authoritarian, technocratic, opaque, single-mindedly in pursuit of export-led growth at whatever cost. The new direction of evolving change is toward a more open, decentred, accountable, and transparent state model" (p. 2). The remainder of this paper will examine whether this new direction is visible in Taiwan, and the conditions that may be facilitating or retarding the transition. We will argue that Taiwan's evolving governance cannot be understood without taking into account simultaneously the peculiar territorial preoccupations of the state on the one hand, and the transterritorial character of its emerging civil society.

Constitutional Reform and Territorial Adjustments
Increasing competition in a global economy, uncertain relations with the People's Republic of China, rising demands for social justice, and competing interests of a segmented public are shaping the agenda of rivaling political parties in Taiwan. One aspect that has received at least temporary bipartisan support is constitutional reform. While there remain many controversial issues to be ironed out, the virtual elimination, or at least significant weakening of the provincial level of government seems certain. Both the ruling Kuomintang (KMT) and the largest opposition party, Minchintang or the Democratic Progressive Party (DPP), agree that for Taiwan there is currently one level too many in its government, although their reasons and motivations for its elimination may not be the same.

Currently there are four levels of government in Taiwan: the national, the provincial, the county/city, and the local level of sub-cities, villages and towns. Two cities, Taipei and Kaohsiung, are under the direct control of the Executive Yuan, a national body. The national level of government is known as the Republic of China (ROC) which has actual jurisdiction over Taiwan Province, the Jinmen and the Mazu islands, and until recently has always claimed jurisdiction over all of China proper. The two islands are part of the Fujian Province which is governed by the People's Republic of China (PRC) that claims jurisdiction over all of China, including the territories governed by the ROC. Except for Taipei and Kaohsiung and the two islands of Fujian that are beyond the jurisdiction of the Taiwan provincial government, there is a complete overlap of territories governed by the national and the provincial levels. The third level comprises 16 counties and 5 cities. The lowest level of government includes more than three hundred sub-cities, villages and towns. The chief executives of all levels of government are elected, although legal charges and rumors of corruption and other election irregularities abound.

The proposed constitutional reform which was to be discussed in the National Assembly in July 1999 consisted of the following:

1. At the local level: townships and villages will remain as the two tiers of local government. Their heads will not be elected as they are now, but instead will be appointed. Likewise, counties and cities will remain, but the authority of their heads will expand (e.g. they may appoint heads of villages and towns). Both the ruling KMT and the DPP thought this restructuring would free the parties from their symbiotic relations with, if not dependence on, underworld forces. The latter also saw an opportunity to seize power from the entrenched local control of the ruling party. However, the unexpected landslide victory of the DPP in city and county elections in late 1997 has given the Kuomintang second thoughts about letting mayors of cities and counties appoint local heads of villages and towns since, up to now, 95% of these local heads are KMT members.

2. At the regional level: regardless which of the two terms, either "eliminate" or "freeze," is used, the provincial level of government will be significantly reduced in power, if not totally eliminated. The governorship, which is currently an elected office, will disappear. The reason why the pro-Taiwan independence DPP is in favor of eliminating this level of government is obvious. Since the territorial state and the Taiwan province share almost the same boundaries, the elimination of the province is *ipso facto* declaring Taiwan an independent state. In addition, the prospect of diminishing the rising influence of Governor Song Chu-yu without much effort on their part is enticing enough. As to why the Kuomintang supports this provision, there are several different views. One holds that the size of the provincial territory is too large for the central state's comfort which has led to the fear of the Yeltsin effect. Another view holds that Lee Tenghui, President and Chairman of the KMT, has long harbored a desire for independence, and achieving it symbolically through Constitutional Reform without confronting the issue directly is certainly a good strategy. A third view is more personal and somewhat clandestine. This view holds that the current governor of Taiwan is, to say the least, not among the favorite sons of the President. Clipping Song's wings is said to be the real motivation behind restructuring.

3. At the central level: greater centralization of power, especially the system of dual leadership involving the president and the head of the Executive Yuan, will weaken the authority of the Legislative Yuan. The head of the Executive Yuan is to be nominated by the President without the consent of the Legislative Yuan, which is contrary to the present constitutional requirement. The expansion of presidential power in the proposed Constitutional Reform endorsed by both the Kuomintang and the DPP has been the centre of debates among scholars.

What purpose does the proposed structural change and its accompanying change of power relations between the hierarchical units serve? Ostensibly, changes at the local level are expected to reduce the currently rampant local election fraud and penetration of underworld figures into officialdom. And, eliminating the provincial level will reduce government expenditure. Finally, it is argued that greater centralization will make the state more effective, both in terms of increasing economic competitiveness and meeting social needs.

Although one can certainly question whether or not these stated purposes would actually be served by the proposed changes, we would like to relate these here to the "new politics" envisioned by Friedmann above.

New Structure, Old Politics

The long period of Chinese immigration and land cultivation in Taiwan culminated in 1886 when the Qing Dynasty made it a province and thus brought it under a singular and comprehensive political governance. However, since the province was ceded to Japan following Qing's defeat in 1895, it is more meaningful to regard the Japanese occupation period as providing the foundation for developing subsequent urban governance. Although Japan restructured Taiwan's administration several times, all versions reflected a top-down framework originating from the colonial Governor, and served the purposes of Japanese political and military control. Similarly, the current administrative structure of Taiwan, set up by the ROC after the Second World War, is a top-down system of control. Though clearly outdated, the structure is so tied to entrenched political interests and local factions, that it has proved extremely difficult to change.

On the other hand, global restructuring and changes in international geo-politics as well as domestic challenges are exerting pressures on the once successful "developmental state." Credited with the post-Second World War "economic miracle," the Taiwan state finds it increasingly difficult to cope with the demands of the new century. One embarrassing example is the so-called Regional Operations Centers project, Taipei's bid for "world-city" status. Due to barriers created by uncertain Mainland-Taiwan relations, the project has not progressed very far since its announcement. Additionally, conflicts between central and local concerns over environmental protection and economic development, and over inequities in access to public services and revenue generation authorities, have led to serious confrontations in domestic politics. In other words, the developmental state model no longer suffices, and the inefficiency of state policy implementation has reached crisis proportions.

Contradictions between traditional nation-state identity and liberal democratic ideology characterize current Taiwan politics. State ineptness has made it impossible to insist on the central government as the hegemonic core carrying the imagery of the nation-state. Whatever political democracy within the developmental state gained after years of persistent struggles guided by liberal ideology, the people of Taiwan suddenly awakened to find the nation-state imagery disintegrating under the simultaneous pressures of globalization and localism. Excluded from the United Nations and most international organizations, and officially recognized by only a handful of Third World nations, the ROC is hard pressed to maintain its status as a sovereign state without declaring independence. Yet, the collective identity of Chinese nationhood, albeit under challenge, still predominates on both sides of the Taiwan strait. This national identity, trapped in an historical framework of territoriality, is driving those who regard themselves as Chinese to pursue some sort of unification between the PRC and the ROC states. Uneven economic development and the varying extent and form of incorporation into the global economy, exert complex cross-pressures on both governments. In Taiwan, global connections and international rejections, economic, if precarious, success, liberal ideology though still limited, and historical circumstances, have combined to produce a widespread localized identity. A new nationhood is being consciously constructed with a clear intention to claim the territorial state.

Accompanying economic growth in past decades has been the gradual decline in the quality of public living environment. Both have facilitated the reemergence of a civil society. People have been mobilized in a variety of ways and on a variety of issues, venting anger, seeking redress, and formulating their different visions of the future. Housing movements, environmental movements, community movements, and movements of women, native peoples, gays and lesbians, etc., either mutually penetrating or exclusive, are all mired in the mixed soil of class, nationality, ethnicity and religion. Although chaotic and fraught with potential problems, the situation gives hope for the development of a civil society with multiple publics which may find expression in a "new politics."

New Structure, New Politics

What can be done with the current territorial governance structure to provide a framework for dealing with the cumulative yearnings for a new politics by the nascent civil society? There must be many possibilities. We outline below some minimal concerns any proposal must meet.

1. The creation of municipal units small enough to allow for grass-roots community participation, and representation of divergent local cultures. This idea of small municipalities with small numbers of people is traceable to Lao-zi's ideal. Small does not necessarily mean homogeneous. But boundaries of territories that have been artificially drawn, and people deliberately pulled apart by the colonial government's "divide and rule" policy can be restored or readjusted. The Hakka people in southern Taiwan is a example.

2. Any gerrymandering must be done in a transparent and open process of competition based on the criteria of social efficiency, equity, and responsiveness to people's needs and desires (Friedmann 1997, 2-3). The "new politics" is predicated on the rule of law. While Taiwan is not lawless, justice is not blind, unfortunately. The close ties between political power and law enforcement are so obvious that they are taken for granted. Experience has shown that the local community can be effectively mobilized to influence some government decisions and to right some wrongs. A transparent and open process of decision-making is critical for encouraging community participation and the formation of a civil society.

3. Using similar criteria of evaluation, some existing counties and cities may be elevated to the status of province to allow for more suitable development. For example, East Taiwan can be targeted for the regional development of tourism and conservation; and an autonomous region of indigenous peoples seems to be long overdue. It is this level of government that is most capable of utilizing institutional strengths to adjust to the exigencies of the global economy and maintain competitiveness. Mechanisms need to be put in place to reduce inequities in allocation and urban-rural inequality.

4. The central government's primary responsibility will be to encourage and facilitate interregional cooperation while respecting local autonomy. Its symbolic value is far more important than its actual power. The central government exists without being obtrusive. At the present historical juncture, we depart from many colleagues in a call

to bring the central government's role closer to Lao-zi's, rather than to Confucian ideals (Cheng and Rosett 1991, 157-160). Putting it simply, while the latter relies on the benevolence of the ruler, the former asks only to leave the people to govern themselves.

Our discussions above which contrast the old politics of the developmental state with the new politics of the emerging civil society represent a strategy of writing rather than a prescriptive cure. We do not intend to suggest a new norm divorced from the political realities of Taiwan but simply to point out that the proposed Constitutional Reform is irrelevant, if not contrary, to the spirit of the new politics. The source of our hesitance is the realization that first, the nascent civil society in Taiwan is still too weak to support any program of systemic change at the national level. Furthermore, such a program requires careful analysis of new political practices, as well as interventions into current practices, and should not be merely a proclamation of normative or even utopian standards. The nation-state ideology and the logic of the developmental state, though obsolete, are still dominant in Taiwan and underlie its politics. The policies emanated from these twin pillars have given rise to numerous social movements and acts of citizen resistance, as well as seemingly endless struggle between unification and independence, an issue which has little to do with the realities of everyday life.

As the developmental state loses its raison d'être, it cannot hold on to its previous autonomy, and must give way to meaningful interaction with an emerging multi-public civil society. Taiwan, faced with uncertain U.S.-China relations in international geo-politics, and an identity crisis perpetuated by an outdated nation-state ideology, seems especially ripe for discussions of a new form of territorial governance. The urgency is indicated by the frequency of conferences organized around the issue by both government agencies and academic institutions. Taiwan's participation in the global flows of capital, goods, information and people creates pressures for a change in state behavior as well as new opportunities for local movements of resistance and reform. The social destruction caused by the economic havoc of globalization is eliciting a plethora of citizen responses, including a demand for more fundamental changes in state and civil society interaction. Structural readjustment provides the physical framework for political practices, and we have pointed out that the proposed readjustment is contrary to the practices of an open, decentred, accountable and transparent post-developmental state model. However, the discussion of territorial governance is incomplete without, at least, taking the character of the reemerging civil society into consideration.

The character and form of this increasingly urban civil society will be effected by the opening-up of Taiwan to international transactions. In particular, the increasing movement of Taiwanese to other parts of the Pacific Rim is having a pronounced effect. In the next section we discuss these developments.

The Emergence of a Transterritorial Society

In a critique of international relations theory, John Agnew (1994) warned against what he calls "the territorial trap." Agnew questioned the validity of the three geographical assumptions of the state: states as fixed units of sovereign space, the domestic/foreign polarity, and states as "containers" of societies. He argued for historicizing the relationship between state and geography. The reification of state territorial spaces as fixed units of secure sovereign space within which society dwells has blinded many to the increasing global fragmentation of daily life, and the growing importance of societies not contained within the state. The problematic relationship between the territorial state and society is not as uncommon as one may think, although here we focus only on a discussion of the Chinese case (Cheng and Katz 1998).

Transterritorial migration is certainly not a new phenomenon. What is new, however, is the intense interconnectedness of individuals' lives across territories claimed by different states and other levels of government. It is commonplace to observe that although the physical existence of individuals is still spatially bound, the meaning of the phrase "one can't be at both places at the same time" is becoming very restricted. The multidirectional flows of labor, goods and capital have combined to make locally accessible images, things and services whose origins are hardly traceable. However, the vast development in transportation and communication has greatly facilitated the maintenance of personal relations and networks across physical borders. These dual aspects of globalization have made transterritorialism a way of life. Nowhere is this more obvious than in the city-regions of the Pacific, and Taipei is a clear example.

A special Chinese term was coined in Taipei about a decade ago to describe the transterritorial, and specifically transnational existence of some Chinese. "Kongzhong feiren" or "trapeze artists" are residents of multiple places, often with at least dual citizenship and carrying passports of different countries. Unlike their previous migrant fellow countrymen or spouses who remained at home in earlier times, they tended to have families, friends and associates interconnected in varying degrees on both sides of the Pacific. Kongzhong feiren participate in the economic, political and social lives of both places. Not only do they contribute monies to organizations of both places, including transnational NGOs, but they also help raise monies from one place for organizations located in the other. The government of Taiwan as well as that of the People's Republic of China have always given formal recognition to their dual status by allocating seats in their respective parliaments or congresses for their representatives. How these representatives have been determined, however, remains a guarded secret to outsiders.

Transnationalism, a level of transterritorialism, is not without controversy in Taiwan. Mayor Chen Shui-bian of Taipei, for example, was forced to let go of his respected transportation chief because of the latter's dual citizenship. After considerable debate, the Legislative Yuan passed a law placing restrictions on dual citizens' participation even in the academic and non-strategic research areas. The law was, however, quickly amended to exempt the highly trained professionals and scientists who are considered indispensible for Taiwan's growth in an increasingly competitive global economy. It would be interesting to see if entrance into world organizations such as the World Trade Organization will lead to a challenge of this and other similar practices of exclusion.

The rise of transnational living is generating worldwide concerns. After a recent *Los Angeles Times* report of an elected local official in New York running for an office in another country, an immediate reaction came through the editorials and letters from readers. They testified to the prevalence of dual citizenship among U.S. citizens and concerns for national security, the demise of nationalism, and social and economic justice. What does citizenship mean in a globalized world? What are the rights and obligations of a global citizen? What are reasonable claims of the territorial state on its citizens? To what extent does nationality and national origin matter in the 21st century? "Who is Us?" appears to be the question of the day (Agnew 1994).

Signs are everywhere that a transterritorial society vis-à-vis territorial states and a supra-state system is emerging. Though sectorally fragmented by class, race, gender, age, environmental concerns, etc., these communities once thought to be contained within states are forming international ties. Some are themselves being transformed into transnational organizations, even as they struggle for local, place-centred justice or compete for resources from the state.

International NGOs, such as the Red Cross, Amnesty International, Habitat International, and YM/YWCA, have existed for a long time. However, what distinguishes emergent transnational NGOs from these traditional international NGOs is their conscious de-territorialization and global orientation. The distinction is not absolute but significant. We will focus our discussion on the situation in Taiwan.

Transterritorialism, NGOs, and the Taiwan State

A survey on the international linkages of three types of NGOs in Taiwan this year found large differences in the extent and scope of such linkages among women, environmental, and labor organizations. Specifically, four points can be made.

1. All three types of organizations have regular institutional contacts with counterparts outside of Taiwan, although the scope, frequency and intensity of these contacts vary among the types as well as within each type of organizations. Environmental nongovernmental organizations are the ones with the closest ties abroad, followed by women and labor in that order. This pattern is consistent with MacShane's observation (1993) worldwide.

2. Environmental organizations are extremely conscious of their trans-territoriality. As one respondent claims: "Birds don't know which country or province they are feeding and resting at. We work with organizations irrespective of the states who hold jurisdiction over the territories. In fact, you may say that all of us are working together against our respective governments." It is not out of the ordinary for environmentalists in Taiwan to marshal support from various foreign environmental groups and world-renowned environmentalists to pressure the state to adopt or implement certain policies. However, this phenomenon is still relatively new in Taiwan. According to one local environmentalist, "Before we were not willing to ask for help or form alliances with foreign groups because such behavior would be viewed as unpatriotic or even treason. You know, 'gao yang-zhuang' (appealing to foreigners) is a serious accusation. But now we don't care. That is often the only way we can get media attention and get things done."

3. Women's organizations have a plethora of contacts with foreign counterparts but these tend to be sporadic and limited to sharing experiences and discussing common issues at conferences. On questions that have already received worldwide attention, such as child prostitution, international involvement is much stronger. Women's organizations complain that the serious lack of resources from the government hampers their participation outside of Taiwan. They also blame the international community for excluding them due to political pressures from China. With some exception, among the three types of organizations, women's organizations seem the least likely to see themselves as standing opposite to the state. They instead express dismay at the weakening of state ability to maintain order and provide personal safety.

4. Despite many restrictions on labor organizing, Taiwan has a number of labor organizations in addition to those officially recognized. Almost all of them have some organizational contacts abroad, and these loose relations are becoming tighter as three parallel developments progressed. The first has to do with the privatization of formerly state-owned industries which has led to numerous demonstrations and the planned formation of the All-Taiwan Independent Confederation of Labor. The government has said that it would not recognize this new union since there is already the All-China (Taiwan) Confederation of Labor sponsored by the government. Independent unions are looking for support as well as providing support, if only symbolically, to unions in other countries that have gone through similar process. Some Taiwan union leaders went to South Korea last year during their big strike to show labor solidarity.

The second development is taking place across the Pacific in the United States. The AFL-CIO has recently initiated visits to Asian countries, including Taiwan, after some successes in cross-border organizing. Their visits to Taiwan were unpublicized. One of the AFL-CIO representatives said in an interview that they had visited three labor unions including the official one, and are thinking of sending a larger delegation to attend the inaugural ceremony of the unofficial All-Taiwan Confederation in late 1998.

The presence of a large number of foreign workers has been a topic of heated debates in Taiwan, and unions have yet to develop a common position. Their status, work conditions and pay are often left to the market forces. Abuses of foreign workers as well as abuses by foreign workers, whether real or alleged, call for increased regulation by the state and protection by the unions. Yet, lack of understanding of conditions in their countries of origin, cultural and language barriers, etc. have impeded local unions in their organizing efforts. For women foreign workers, there seems to be a strong transnational network of support. The Taiwan node of the Committee for Asian Women Workers (CAW) is an example of the third development.

The uncertain political status of Taiwan and its relationship with mainland China distinguishes it from other sovereign states. Sometimes this is cited by NGOs as barriers to international participation.

Writing in 1993 on the arrival of the new age of internationals, MacShane noted nine "internationals" including bankers, private capitalist, and trade unions; religious, political, electronic and green; as well as governmental and non-governmental, "each exercising a role in world affairs equal to and increasingly more important than that of the nation-state and national institutions of commerce, culture or politics."

(MacShane 1993, 23). Clearly the civil society in Taiwan is mindful of the power of transnationalism and draws on it for support. Linkages to international civil society organizations facilitate the drawing of media coverage, which puts pressure on the nation-state. This strategy is especially helpful to the traditionally neglected and more marginal groups in the society, such as indegenous peoples, and women. However, we must also be mindful of the potential risks that are involved.

Theoretically, a civil society is autonomous to the state. But in most countries recently emerged from authoritarian rule, especially economically less developed countries, this is not the case. The traditional patron-client relationship, the fragile economic base, the lack of a culture that encourages public giving as well as the lack of fundraising know-how, the intention of the state to coopt and control society, and other factors have been cited by various scholars to account for this phenomenon (Diamond 1997). Unable to raise enough funds to carry out their missions, the reliance of Taiwan's NGOs on state funds has brought public suspicions and fostered unhealthy competition. To avoid dependence on the state in order to retain a legitimate critical stance, many NGOs have sought foreign sources of support, ranging from the Ford Foundation to the World Bank.

However, international donors have their own priorities which may not match domestic needs. As a result, some types of NGOs are more likely to receive funds than others. For instance, environmental issues are favored over trade union issues in the current historical juncture. "Gatt refuses to talk to international trade unions about trade and workers' rights, but opens its door to meetings with environmentalists about trade in dolphins. Elephants enjoy a world ban in trade on their tusks but efforts to ban child labor or put an end to the supply of teenage slaves from Asia to the Gulf States come to naught" (MacShane 1993, 24).

Furthermore, within any specific type, donor priorities may also differ from recipient organizations. NGOs often have to compromize and adjust to the exigencies of the international donors, or camouflage their real program intentions to fit international agendas. This need to cater to the current interests of international donor agencies lends some credence to James Petras's scathing critique of NGOs in Latin America (1997). Petras accused these organizations as creations of neoliberal politicians to compete with socio-political movements for the allegiance of local leaders and activist communities. By focusing their activities at the local level, these NGOs severed the links between local struggles and organizations and national/international political movements. Historically Petras may be correct, but the general condemnation of NGOs seems premature. Recent debates within the NGO community testify to this observation. While many NGOs are brokers between local organizations, neoliberal foreign donors and the local free market regimes, not a few are at the forefront of transformational movements.

Several encouraging developments limiting civil society's reliance on the state and international donor agencies are visible in Taiwan. First and foremost is the "diversification" formula adopted by several organizations which puts an upper limit to state funds, usually not more than 20%. Similarly, an effort is made to seek out a larger number of international donor sources from a wider set of countries to avoid dominance by any particular country or agency. Increasing access to internet has greatly expanded the information on international donor agencies, and facilitated organizations to apply for smaller grants from agencies and countries without previous contact.

Second, more and more civil society organizations are beginning to raise funds from their potential constituencies. Most civil society organizations in Taiwan are not based on membership and have not had the experience in large-scale membership drives. Besides the state, they have relied to a large extent on contributions from corporations, other NGOs and NPOs organized as foundations, and individuals. There is now a greater awareness that by cultivating a base of support among a broad constituency, civil society gains greater autonomy as well as elicits deeper member commitment and participation, and ultimately establishes cultural norms that make a "new politics" possible (Diamond 1997, 51-52).

Third, a horizontal and cooperative relationship based on mutual assistance and respect which characterizes the linkage between some Taiwan civil society organizations and their counterparts in Third World countries is emerging. Unlike the donor-recipient relationship which has dominated NGO alliances between the U.S. and Taiwan, this new phenomenon reflects in part the realization of common concerns among peoples of developing countries.

As a continuing process of capital accumulation, globalization has already left millions homeless and foodless in the last decade. Yet it is touted as a panacea to the world's economic problems. In Pacific Asia, the Philippines is probably the country most devastated by this process, or perhaps it is the people there that have been most vocal in their opposition. (People's Campaign 1996). Throughout the 1990s, Filipino NGOs have spearheaded a movement of resistance, and their representative came to share organizing experiences in workshops joined by similar NGOs in Taiwan. About half a dozen native people's and women's organizations talked about institutionalizing their cooperative activities in a common resistance against globalization.

Conclusion

The transterritorial character of daily life and of civil society binds global and local issues as well as constituencies. As a Chinese diaspora continues, and destinations diverge, networks expand, and the flow of information is strengthened with personal touches. By simultaneous participation in different civil societies contained within nation-states, civil societies are themselves transnationalized. Such societies, no longer containable within a territorial state, can strenthen the role of the civil society vis-à-vis its state in any particular country, Taiwan included.

References

Agnew, J. 1994. The Territorial Trap: the geographical assumptions of international relations theory? *Review of International Political Economy* 1,1: 53-80.

Cheng, L. and M. Katz. 1998. Migration and the Diaspora Communities. *Culture and Society in the Asia-Pacific*. Edited by R. Maidment and C. Mackerras. London: Routledge. 65-87.

Cheng, L. and A. Rosett. 1991. Contract with a Chinese Face: Socially Embedded Factors in the Transformation from Hierarchy to Market, 1978-1989. *Journal of Chinese Law*. 5, 2 (Fall): 143-244.

Craig, G. and M. Mayo. 1995. *Community Empowerment*. London: Zed.

Diamond, L. 1997. *Civil Society and the Development of Democracy*. Estudio/ Working paper 1997/101. Madrid: Juan March Institute.

Friedmann, J. 1997. An Approach to Research on the Territorial Governance of Urban Regions in the Asia-Pacific Realm. Unpublished memo to participants of the Intercity Networks in Asia-Pacific Region. 23 May.

MacShane, D. 1993. The New Age of the Internationals. *New Statesman & Society*. 30 April: 23-26.

People's Campaign Against Imperialist Globalization. 1996. *Globalization: Displacement, Commodification and Modern-Day Slavery of Women*. Quezon City, Philippines: Gabriela.

Rozario, S. 1997. Development and Rural Women in South Asia: The Limits of Empowerment and Conscientization. *Bulletin of Concerned Asian Scholars*. 29, 4 (October-December): 45-53.

Scholte, J.A. 1996. The Geography of Collective Identities in a Globalizing World? *Review of International Political Economy*. 3, 4 (Winter):565-607.

Sivaramakrishnan, K.C. 1996. Urban Governance: Changing Realities, in *Preparing for the Urban Future: Global Pressures and Local Forces*. Edited by M. Cohen et al. Washington, D.C.: Woodrow Wilson Center, 225-241.

Storper, M. 1998. Civil Society: Three Ways into a Problem. *Cities for Citizens*. Edited by M. Douglas and J. Friedmann. Chichester: John Wiley & Sons. 239-246.

World Bank. 1994. *Governance—The World Bank's Experience*. Washington, D.C.: World Bank.

TERRY MCGEE

Governing Mega-Urban Regions: The Case of Vancouver

I n the introductory paper of this collection, Friedmann engages a central issue of urban governance—what criteria should be used for assessing the performance of cities? He proposes three sets: governance, management and outcomes. At the same time, he is careful to argue that these criteria should not be used for the measurement of comparative performance between cities. Rather he hopes that they will serve as an agenda for citizen involvement and action.

While there will undoubtedly be some disagreement over these criteria, his essay raises a central issue that I think must be engaged. How will the criteria for city performance relate to the wider urban region of which most cities form a functional part? It is by now well understood that the processes of urbanization lead to the creation of large urban regions often composed of many cities which together form an "integrated urban space."[1] Such regions stretch for many kilometers in the case of Tokyo (up to 50 kilometers) encompassing many political jurisdictions that exhibit considerable variation in the extent to which they satisfy the criteria of "good governance." The effect of this is to threaten the "sustainability" of other parts of the same region. For instance, if city A in the urban region fails to enforce "industrial pollution" laws, the industrial waste deposited in rivers may flow into other city spaces where industrial pollution laws have already been adopted. This failure to cooperate is the kind of issue which so intrigues Putnam and his collaborators (1993) and lead him to focus on the role of institutions in facilitating voluntary cooperation on such problems.[2] Friedmann is not unaware of this dilemma but clearly argues that it is a matter of priorities. In the absence of regional government, the best space for the application of the criteria for good governance is the political territory of the city.

Although the logic of this position is unarguable, it does not automatically mean that efforts to develop "regional governance" should be discarded. The problem of the "mega-urban commons" still remains and presents the need to develop effective management at the regional level. Indeed, I would argue that the two governance processes—of city and region—should proceed concurrently. I am fully aware that their synchronization will be difficult, involving a careful articulation of local and regional needs. However, their articulation is essential in producing the sustainable, livable, productive, tolerant, and caring outcomes that Friedmann suggests.

This paper describes the case of the Vancouver urban region in the Province of British Columbia, Canada, as an example of an articulated process of city and regional governance. It shows that city regions can develop a kind of strategic planning that permits progress to be made at both scales toward "good governance" outcomes, and at the same time, reinforce the competitive strength of an urban region within the networks of global cities.

Vancouver in its Regional Context

As a background to this description of governance, it is important to stress that Vancouver is part of a wide region of "geographical affinity." Thus, there are three geographical regions in which Vancouver is nested. The largest region stretches from southern Oregon to the ski resort of Whistler (120 km north of Vancouver). This includes Metropolitan Portland, Seattle and Vancouver as its major urban cores and has been termed "Cascadia" (Schnell and Hamer 1993; Edgington 1995; Pivo 1996). Within this wider region, the main urban focus is the urban corridor which stretches from Eugene, Oregon, through Seattle-Tacoma and on to the Greater Vancouver area up to the ski resort centre of Whistler (see Map 1). This corridor is linked by a major international highway, intensive air traffic routes and a railroad linkage characterized by daily trips. These three major urban cores act as the gateways for commodity and passenger movements to the Western region of Canada and the U.S. An increasing proportion of business in the region is carried out with Asia Pacific countries. Almost half of its exports go to this region and urban foreign investment from Asian Pacific countries is a major source of capital. But not all exports are raw materials. This corridor is also the site of three of the largest world multinationals: Boeing and Microsoft in Seattle and Nike and Hewlett-Packard in Portland. Vancouver is now popularly known as Hollywood North and is host to the second largest number of movie productions in North America. It is no coincidence that these industries represent the leading edge of the post-industrial era, entertainment leisure, transportation and information. This Asia Pacific linkage has been further reinforced by the movements of new migrants from Asia Pacific

Map 1: Cascadia and the Pacific Northwest Economic Region (Edgington, 1995)

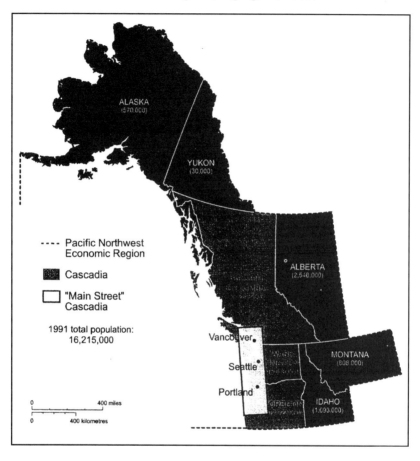

nations, most markedly to the central part of the Greater Vancouver area. Mobility within the urban corridor is high; over 1.4 million American tourists visit B.C. each year by land (most from the urban corridor Main Street Cascadia) and over 1.0 million Canadians visit the U.S. from B.C.

The second region with which Vancouver is closely integrated is the extended metropolitan region (EMR) of the southern mainland of B.C. which encompasses approximately 50 percent of the province's population and generates more than 50 percent of the GDP of the province/ state.[4] Vancouver forms part of this extended region of urban interaction which stretches across the Georgia Strait to Vancouver Island and includes the provincial capital Victoria and a string of towns that stretch along the north-south island highway as far north as Parksville. In the south, the EMR follows the IR 5 south to Bellingham (see Map 2). One of the world's largest ferry systems moves people and goods between the internal routes of Nanaimo, Victoria, Vancouver. Local air transport flies every hour and the IR 5 throughway links Bellingham with Vancouver.

The final regional scale is the urban region of Vancouver. Today, this is defined as the Greater Vancouver Regional District (GVRD), consisting of a partnership of municipalities and two electoral areas that make up the metropolitan area of Greater Vancouver. One municipality outside the GVRD takes advantage of some services offered by the District. In 1996, this area contained 1.9 million people. The major part of the population is focused on the City of Vancouver, with an estimated population of 514,007 in 1996. Together with the adjacent municipalities of Burnaby (179,209), New Westminster (49,350), North Vancouver City (41,475), North Vancouver District (81,418), West Vancouver (41,882) and Richmond (148,867) make up 67 percent of the total population. The GVRD is expected to grow by another million to 3 million by 2020 (see Map 3).

**Map 2: Boundaries of the Greater Vancouver Regional District,
Municipalities and Districts (Wynn and Oke 1992)**

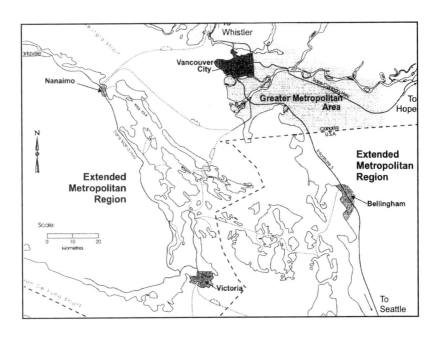

Map 3: Vancouver Extended Metropolitan Region

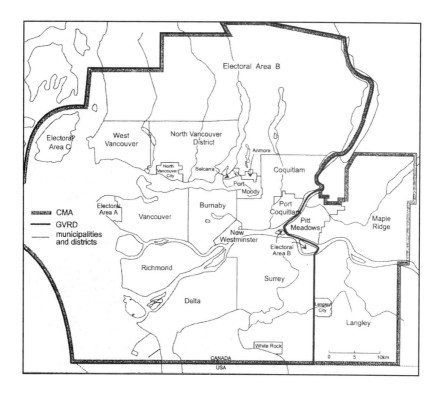

Vancouver as Part of the Asia Pacific Urban System

The Vancouver urban region has a certain distinctiveness in the group of city regions that are presented in this volume. First, it is important to stress that the Vancouver urban region is of fairly recent origin. In the early part of the nineteenth century, at a time when many other sub-global cities had been established for centuries, Vancouver was still a "native place" in which Indian bands controlled most of the territory. The small European trading ports clung to the edge of the rainforest and it was not until 1867 that British Columbia entered the Canadian Federation. From that time onwards, Vancouver became defined by its role as the port and principal urban centre of a "staples frontier" involving the export of salmon, timber and pulp and minerals. Vancouver's economy was primarily oriented to servicing this frontier. Finance, retailing and small industries such as machine repair were all dedicated to this purpose. This led to a highly dualistic class structure in which the elites that governed and managed B.C. consisted primarily of the managers and owners of the large corporate entities that controlled the economy while the working class labored in the timber mills, the mines and the clerical jobs of the service economy. The governing class was highly concentrated in the core of Vancouver city; the working class, for the most part, settled on the city's edge, shading into the resource frontier beyond it (see Wynn and Oke 1992).

Since 1945, Vancouver's increasing urbanization and the growth of producer services have fueled a spatial expansion of the built environment into nearby agricultural areas such as the Fraser valley. Today the built environment of the Vancouver urban region is very new. Approximately 80 percent of the commercial and residential buildings have been built since the end of the Second World War. This newness provides an architectural setting which encourages innovation and willingness to accept change on the part of the urban managers. This is seen as a necessary quality in the building of strategic networks (see Hutton 1988).

Much of this expansion has been driven by surging population growth, particularly net international migration which increased its share of population growth in the Vancouver urban region from 33 percent in the early 1980s to 59 percent during 1991-1994. Future projections of population growth suggest the Vancouver urban region will reach 3 million by 2021.

Of course, this rapid population growth has been experienced by other cities discussed in the Asia Pacific region. But the distinctiveness of Vancouver (which it shares with Sydney) is the shift from European migrants to flows of Asian migration from Hong Kong, Taiwan, the People's Republic of China, the Philippines and Korea who today make up an important component of the total population.

A second trend relates to the gender aspects of these demographic trends. Ley and his co-authors say: "The radical transformations in the types of work that individuals do, the number of workers per household, the work within households, have led to a radical redistribution of demographic groups in the internal space of the GVRD. In 1960, the GVRD seemed to conform to the model of North American cities where the central city was made up of renters, ethnic minorities, the elderly, the poor, the single and the marginalized as well as those living sub-cultural lifestyles. Around the stretched suburbs characterized by simple family households" (Ley, Hiebert and Pratt 1992, 24). But in the next 20 years, a growing diversity of household types have emerged, especially the increase of of single person rented households which is partly related to the increasing cost of single-family housing in the core of the GVRD.

These demographic trends are partially reflected in labor force trends, where there has been a dramatic increase in the services sector as well as a continuing growth in size of the manufacturing and construction sector. While the more general reasons for this restructuring of urban labor force have been well researched, the specific causes in Vancouver are more complex. Many commentators feel that the turning point in the Vancouver economy occurred with the decision to hold the Expo of 1986 which occurred at the end of the recession of the early 1980s. The decision of the provincial government to invest in major public works, a recovery in "staple" prices, the continuing investment in gateway facilities, including "a cruise ship facility," new container facilities and the extension of the airport have made Vancouver a major competitive destination for international tourism. Thus a number of conventions held in greater Vancouver increased from 291 (with 117,000 delegates) in 1981 to 358 in 1995 (with 164,000 delegates). The number of overnight visitors increased from 5.9 million in 1991 to 7.0 million in 1995 and the international visitors (including US) rose from 675,000 to 1.1 million. Other developments include film and television productions in the city. The industrial structure has also changed with an emphasis on consultancy, software development, biotechnology and new innovation industries. Vancouver is becoming a major centre for architectural services and the multi-media industry.

However, these developments have to be modulated by the need to protect the region's unique natural environment, located on the narrow edge between the Rocky Mountains and the Pacific. With commodity exports in decline, a threatened resource base, and a shift to producer services, there is an emerging tension as British Columbia and Vancouver position themselves to become one of the major tourist amenity regions in the world.

Administration, Power and Governance

This is the context in which this tension must be negotiated in the urban region of Vancouver. The political units which are members of the Greater Vancouver Regional District (GVRD)[5] are administered by elected bodies for each political unit. There is no ward system; the political parties that control the local councils, although not directly aligned with provincial parties, represent a broad coalition of pro-business groups and more socially concerned labor-supported parties. At present, pro-business parties control most councils. But the planning system operating them allows for opposition to be represented through a process of public participation required by provincial statutes. In addition to zoning regulation, municipal councils are responsible for service provision, including fire, police and garbage collection and disposal.

Given that there are three tiers of government—province, regional district and municipality—it is obvious that there is considerable scope for conflict among them, particularly over growth goals and the allocation of funds for regional initiatives. The existence of a regional authority which can deal with the multiple issues that inevitably arise with the emergence of a large urban region in a confined space is seen as providing a coordinating capacity that emphasizes partnerships between the several levels of government as well as among the different municipalities belonging to the GVRD.

For this reason, I will now focus on aspects of strategic planning for land use, economic development, and transportation by the GVRD which has prepared a Livable Region Strategic Plan for 2021. The participation effort which, while it did not incorporate all the elements of citizen involvement that Friedmann's criteria would demand, nevertheless accomplished a great deal before the plan itself was approved in 1996. The plan has five main objectives:

1. The densification of population within the central metropolitan region of Vancouver, Burnaby, New Westminster, Richmond, and North Vancouver.
2. The growth of regional town centres in the New Westminster, Lonsdale, Surrey, Richmond, Metrotown, Coquitlam, Langley and Haney.
3. Implementing a mass transit system that will link these major centres through a private-public partnership.
4. The commitment of more than two-thirds of the GVRD's land base to a green zone that will protect watersheds, parks, ecologically important areas, working forests and farmland from urban development. At present, half of the region's developable land has been designated as green space.
5. The GVRD will continue to implement environmentally acceptable policies of waste removal and treatment, water provision and pollution control.

The implementation of this strategic plan is by no means an easy task and involves continuing negotiations between the province, districts and municipalities with which the GVRD has to operate in partnership. At the same time, each of the municipalities has its own strategic plan that must be accommodated into the overall vision for the region. However, over the last five years, the Province of British Columbia has developed a series of planning measures designed to put in place planning procedures aimed at reducing conflict between the various levels of government within all regional districts in the Province. This

Growth Strategies Act was introduced as an amendment to the Municipal Act in October 1995 and is administered by the Ministry of Municipal Affairs for British Columbia. In line with it, local governments (i.e., regional districts and municipalities) are required to prepare three planning instruments:

a. A Regional Growth Strategy (RGS) that commits a local government for the next 20 years to a regional "vision." This statement about the future of the region must include social, economic, and environmental objectives; population and employment projections; and proposed actions intended to meet the needs of future residents in relation to five sectors:

   • housing
   • transportation
   • regional district services
   • parks and natural areas
   • economic development.

   The Regional Growth Strategy is prepared in consultation with the general public, First Nations organizations, and interested groups, including school districts, regional health boards and regional service delivery organizations. Once the RGS is completed, it must go to public hearings. An intergovernmental committee (IAC) is then set up to advise on the development of the strategy and help coordinate provincial and local government involvement. This committee is comprised of senior staff of local governments as well as representatives of the pertinent provincial ministries. Finally, the RGS process provides an opportunity for more than one regional district to be involved. The Regional Growth Act recognizes that districts throughout the province will have different capacities to develop RGSs, and gives them some latitude to move at a slower pace; it also provides some facilitation in the preparation of their RGS. The second stage of the Regional Growth Strategy process is the submission of the regional growth strategy plans to all local governments within the regional districts as well as to adjacent districts. All parties to the bylaw have no more than 120 days to lodge objections and, if mediation fails to produce results, the province may initiate a binding settlement process by arbitration.

b. The next phase is one of implementation in which municipalities have up to two years to prepare a Regional Context Statement (RCS) which forms part of their Official Community Plan that sets out the relationship between the Regional Growth Strategy and the municipality's plan. The RGS must be acceptable to the regional district; otherwise, the same dispute resolution processes as before are put in place.

c. The final phase is an Implementation Agreement (IA) which is, in effect, a partnership agreement between the regional district and various levels of government that spells out how the Regional Growth Strategy will be carried out. Since this process is still very new (1995), its impact is difficult to gauge. In the case of the Vancouver Regional District, which already had a RGS in place, it has been moving forward quite rapidly, despite objections by three municipalities (Burnaby, Surrey and Richmond) over some aspects of the RGS.

Regional Growth Strategy Plans are generally presented in terms of broad conceptual statements concerning land use, housing, transportation, regional district services, parks, natural areas and economic development. They incorporate the principles set forth in the GVRD vision but do not have formal binding capacity until they become by-laws of the Municipal Act. There appears to be ample opportunity for negotiation in the process between various levels of government, but clearly there must be a commitment to the broad principles adopted by the Greater Vancouver Regional District.

It may be argued, therefore, that the institutional organization of the urban region of Vancouver represents a valid response to the development of a governance and management systems of urban regions which now possesses the capacity to produce outcomes of a good city governance and management. It must also be recognized that the relationships between regional governance and municipal governments are still evolving. At the time of writing, the Provincial government of British Columbia is in the middle of revising the Municipal Act to the effect that municipalities must now take on many more responsibilities than before. Some public groups have argued that the low voter turnouts at municipal elections could be remedied by the introduction of a ward system. Although the ward system might seem to offer greater opportunities for local participation, it may also upset the delicate balance that now exists between, on the one hand, the pro-business parties that dominate the elected city councils under present city-wide elections and thus also in the regional authority and more locally entrenched groups, on the other. It would also completely destroy the achievements that the GVRD has made over the last 30 years.

Conclusion

This examination of the governance and management features of the GVRD illustrates that it is possible, and indeed, necessary to develop organizational responses to the emergence of urban regions. Elsewhere, I have argued that, in an era of increasing global competition, strategic planning for "livable" and "sustainable" urban regions is needed to make city-regions more competitive (see McGee and Robinson 1991). Vancouver's role as a gateway, tourist centre and attractive location for professional immigrants further emphasizes the importance of creating an "amenable" city-region. The process of creating "good governance" in Vancouver has been characterized by emphasis upon municipal partnerships, growth management, creating a livable region, and increasing choices for the regions' inhabitants in transport, work, and recreation within a framework that works with market forces, not against them.

It is also clear that this process of creating regional governances involves a delicate system of checks and balances between the various levels of government and other sectors such as business and citizen action groups. This is tied together with a vision of a livable city region in the twenty-first century which accommodates the interaction between the territorial scales which are discussed in the introduction to this paper.

It would be a mistake to suggest that the Vancouver model of regional governance is transferable in its present form to countries in Asia where urban regions have much bigger populations, large numbers of poor people, and institutional configurations of governance that have much in common with Putnam's Southern Italian regions. Even so, they, too, will have to explore ways of articulating local urban with regional governance. Indeed, it can be argued that if they do not, the conditions of urban life will be unsustainable in the long run. As Vancouver demonstrates, a government for mega-urban regions that balances local with regional concerns is not only possible but a requirement.

Notes

[1]   Discussions of mega-urban formations include Gottmann (1961), Hall (1977). In the Asian context, see Ginsburg, et al. (eds., 1991), Fuchs et al. (eds., 1994), McGee and Robinson (eds., 1995), Lo and Yeung (eds., 1996).

[2]   The work of Putnam (1993) has been credited with reviving the role of "collective action" in resolving problems of individual differences. He argues that "Voluntary cooperation is easier in a community that has inherited a substantial stock of social capital in the forms of norms of reciprocity and networks of social engagement" (p.167).

³   The term was popularized by Garreau in 1991. For further discussion, see Edgington (1995).
⁴   The term "Extended Metropolitan Region" is discussed in Ginsburg, et al. (1991).
⁵   The GVRD has an excellent website with up-to-date factual information on the Vancouver region: http://www.gvrd.bc.ca

References

Economist. 1994. Welcome to Cascadia. 21 May, 52.

Edgington, D. 1995. Trade, Investment and the New Regionalism: Cascadia and its Economic Linkages with Japan. *Canadian Journal of Regional Science*. Vol. XVIII:3.

Friedmann, J. 1999. The Common Good: Assessing the Performance of Cities. This issue.

Fuchs, R. et al., eds. 1994. *Mega-City Growth and the Future*. Tokyo: UN University Press.

Garreau, J. 1981. *The Nine Nations of North America*. Boston: Houghton, Mifflin & Co.

Ginsburg, N., B. Koppel and T.G. McGee, eds. 1991. *The Extended Metropolis: Settlement Transition in Asia*. Honolulu: University of Hawaii Press.

Gottman, J. 1961. Megalopolis: The Urbanized Northeastern Seaboard of the United States. New York: The Twentieth Century Fund.

Hall, P. 1977. *The World Cities*. New York: McGraw Hill.

Hutton, T. 1998. *The Transformation of Canada's Pacific Metropolis: A Study of Vancouver*. Montreal: Institute for Research on Public Policy.

Lo, F.-C. and Y.-M. Yeung, eds. 1996. *Emerging World Cities in the Asia Pacific*. Tokyo: UN University Press.

Lewis, W. Arthur. 1955. *The Theory of Economic Growth*. London: Allen and Unwin.

Ley, D., D. Hiebert and G. Pratt. 1992. Time to Grow Up? From Urban Village to World City. *Vancouver and its Region*. Edited by G. Wynn and T. Oke. Vancouver: University of British Columbia Press, 234-266.

McGee, T.G. and I. Robinson, eds.. 1995. *The Mega-Urban Regions of Southeast Asia*. Vancouver: University of British Columbia Press.

Marr, B.E. 1996. The Greater Vancouver Regional District: Its Purpose, Programs and Administrative Structure. Unpublished paper. Vancouver: GVRD.

Pivo, G. 1996. Towards Sustainable Urbanization on Mainstream Cascadia. *Cities*. 13, 5: 339-354.

Putnam, R.D. et al. 1993. *Making Democracy Work: Civic Traditions in Modern Italy*. Princeton, New Jersey: Princeton University Press.

Schnell, P. and J. Hamer. 1993. What is the Future of Cascadia? *Occasional Paper No. 2*. Seattle: Seattle Discovery Institute.

Wynn, G. and T. Oke, eds. 1992. *Vancouver and Its Region*. Vancouver: University of British Columbia Press.

Authors

Lucie Cheng
Graduate School for Social Transformation
Shih-Hsin University
Taipei, Taiwan
or
Department of Sociology
UCLA
Los Angeles, USA

John Friedmann
Professor Emeritus
UCLA
Los Angeles, USA

K.C. Ho
Department of Sociology
National University of Singapore
Singapore

Chu-Joe Hsia
Graduate Institute of Building and Planning
National Taiwan University
Taipei, Taiwan

Toshio Kamo
School of Law
Osaka University
Osaka, Japan

Won Bae Kim
Korean Research Institute of Human Settlements
Seoul, Korea

Terry McGee
Institute of Asian Research
University of British Columbia
Vancouver, Canada

Peter Murphy
Faculty of the Built Environment
University of New South Wales
Sydney, Australia

Dong-Ho Shin
Department of Regional Development
Hannam University
Taejon, Korea

Chung-Tong Wu
Faculty of the Built Environment
University of New South Wales
Sydney, Australia

Publications
of the Institute of Asian Research

Asia Pacific Report
The newsletter is published biannually and distributed to Friends of Asian Research. Annual membership fee is $10. Editor: Eleanor Laquian.

Design for the New Millennium:
The C.K. Choi Building for the Institute of Asian Research
Edited by Eleanor Laquian (1996). Hardcover $29.95; paperback $19.95. *Design for the New Millennium* marks the official inauguration of the C.K. Choi Building and takes up three themes. The first section, *Campus Greening*, deals with the design and processes to create an environmentally sensitive building. The second section of the book, *Institution Building*, deals with the history of the Institute, fund raising, new organization and structure, and research activities focusing on the culture, history and development of Asian societies. The final section, *Global Networking*, describes how the Institute and UBC are pursuing their vision and mandate to internationalize their programs with linkages and joint research projects with institutions in the Asia Pacific region.

The Empowerment of Asia: Reshaping Global Society
Essays by Alexander Woodside, Paul M. Evans, Jomo K.S., Edward Seidensticker, Sumit Ganguly, Chong-un Kim, and David S.G. Goodman (1996). Paperback, $19.95.
The Empowerment of Asia approaches empowerment from different perspectives. It deals with broad components of the empowerment of Asia and presents evidence of its process at a sub-regional level. The authors emphasize the need to critically evaluate the more macro discourse concerning the empowerment of Asia as it actually occurs at the level of national units.

Joseph Ejercito "Erap" Estrada: The Centennial President
By Aprodicio and Eleanor Laquian (1998). Hc $34.95; pb, $24.95.
The Centennial President is a personal behind-the-scenes account of the exciting campaign that elected Joseph Ejercito "Erap" Estrada as the 13th President of the Republic of the Philippines. The book explains how and why he won the presidency. It details the strategies, the events and the people responsible for Estrada's stunning political victory in the exciting May 1998 elections.

Pacific Encounters: The Production of Self and Other
Edited by Eva-Marie Kröller, Allan Smith, Joshua Mostow and Robert Kramer (1997). Paperback, $19.95.

Pacific Encounters, an excellent collection of essays in the history and theory of discourse, contact, exploration and travel is concerned with how travellers, sojourners and immigrants construct the people and places they find abroad. It also considers the ways those observers and the text they produce are themselves constituted by the process of figuration in which they are implicated. The collection will be of interest to readers in literary studies, geography, history, political sciences, sociology and anthropology.

The Silent Debate: Asian Immigration and Racism in Canada
Edited by Eleanor Laquian, Aprodicio Laquian and Terry McGee (1998) Paperback, $24.95.

The Silent Debate looks at Asian immigration to Canada, particularly to Vancouver and Toronto, and its socio-economic and political impact on Canadian society. It examines these issues from the receiving as well as the sending countries' points of view. In addition, it compares the Canadian experience with those of other countries with large Asian populations such as the United States, Australia and New Zealand.

The World My Mother Gave Me: Asian Women's Perspectives and Perceptions in Literature
Edited by Mandakranta Bose (1998). Paperback, $19.95.

The essays in The World My Mother Gave Me study how women from a range of Asian cultures perceive their world as one they have inherited from their mothers and, further, to speculate on the implications of these perceptions within an intergenerational matrix. Taking writings both by and on women as their material, the authors open a multiplicity of texts to critical analyses whereby they uncover the cultural roots of women's relationships with the world they inhabit.

Prices in Canadian funds. Shipping and handling rates: 1-3 books, $5.00; 4 books and over, $8.00. Canadian orders add 7% GST.

Please direct inquiries to:
UBC Press
6344 Memorial Road
Vancouver, B.C., Canada V6T 1Z2
Tel: (604) 822-5959   Fax: (604) 822-6083
E-mail: orders@ubcpress.ubc.ca